T0114523

A

Certified

Couch Potato's
(Ccp)
View Of The World

By Tony Cotton

Note for Librarians: A cataloguing record for this book is available from Library and Archives Canada at www.collectionscanada.ca/amicus/index-e.html

Printed in Victoria, BC, Canada.

ISBN: 978-1-4251-5214-7 (sc)

ISBN: 978-1-4251-5215-4 (dj)

We at Trafford believe that it is the responsibility of us all, as both individuals and corporations, to make choices that are environmentally and socially sound. You, in turn, are supporting this responsible conduct each time you purchase a Trafford book, or make use of our publishing services. To find out how you are helping, please visit www.trafford.com/responsiblepublishing.html

Our mission is to efficiently provide the world's finest, most comprehensive book publishing service, enabling every author to experience success. To find out how to publish your book, your way, and have it available worldwide, visit us online at www.trafford.com

Trafford rev. 7/02/2009

Trafford
PUBLISHING® www.trafford.com

North America & international
toll-free: 1 888 232 4444 (USA & Canada)
phone: 250 383 6864 ♦ fax: 250 383 6804 ♦ email: info@trafford.com

The United Kingdom & Europe
phone: +44 (0)1865 487 395 ♦ local rate: 0845 230 9601
facsimile: +44 (0)1865 481 507 ♦ email: info.uk@trafford.com

CONTENTS

1. THE HISTORY OF CERTIFIED COUCH POTATOES (CCPS)

"And if you don't like my point of view, tough! That's what FREEDOM is all about. Not political correctness or "entitlement" politics with every little special interest group vying for YOUR tax dollars instead of going where they SHOULD." ...Nick Carter

Contrary to popular belief, you do not have to have a case of "BAD Syndrome" (Broad Ass Disease) or a big helping of "Dunlap" (this is where your belly has 'Dun-Lapped' over your belt buckle). All you have to do to become a card carrying CCP is to be human. We are presently looking into opening a chapter for aliens, but Will Smith and his Men in Black organization have not returned our calls. To be an active member you have to participate in the three following activities: 1) Breathing, 2) Having a pulse, and 3) Responding to stimuli from some form of electronic equipment. If you fail to meet one of the three requirements your status will be moved to the inactive file. If you fail to meet two of the three requirements, this means either you are dead or were elected to the U.S. Senate to replace Strom Thurman for the state of South Carolina.

CCP is the ultimate equal opportunity organization. CCP does not care what your religion is, that is, if you have one. We do not care what sex you sleep with (only requirement here is that your partner is human; this rule may be waived once the alien chapter is up and running), or what your national origin is. Let's face it… In America, the majority of us are boat people; the Native Americans were the first INS agents our ancestors saw. CCP organization is color-blind. There are no white, black, brown, yellow, or red people and there are no African-Americans, Latino-Americans, Asian-Americans or WASPs. There is only one race and it is called Human. Again, this rule may be waived once the alien chapter is up and running.

The CCP organization is the only one in the world that can state, without a doubt, that there is not a job or position in the world that has not been held by, at any given time, a CCP member. We are proud to have members that are garbage men (Notice the word "men." CCP is not a very PC organization. If Toni Cotton was writing this book, it would then be garbage person or whatever), politicians, soldiers, sailors, astronauts, and even a U.S. President or two. Let's face it Gerald Ford was not our most coordinated member. From the outhouses to the penthouse, from the shop floors to the boardrooms, we have proud card carrying members and some not so proud members (these members are still in the closet). We are a force to be reckoned with and now we are going to let our views be heard once and for all, and I don't mean on some infomercial at 2:00 a.m. on channel whatever.

The CCP organization is not a religion, so you do not have to "find" anybody, be it Jesus, Mohammed, Buddha, or whatever. CCP is not a union, so there are no dues, but we represent anyone that wants to join. It is not a political party, but be assured it is a force to be reckoned with on certain issues. It is not a charity (yet) because most of its' members donate to other organizations regularly. CCP is not funded by any State or Federal government agency, "Think Tanks", private industry or foreign governments. It's not that we would turn down the money if offered. We are trying to obtain a charity status with the IRS so that any donations would be tax-free. This is not looking promising because of the alien chapter that we are in the process of opening. If you think the IRS gets upset about money going into banks in the Caymans, you should have seen the expression on their faces regarding banks out of this galaxy.

Most of the world sees members of CCP as the stereotypical couch potato that Hollywood and the TV industry have taken pleasure in creating… you know the ones, BAD Syndrome & Dunlap. We know one group that believed this Hollywood BS and bet their lives on the myth. On September 11, 2001, Osama Bin Laden and his cronies opened that "Industrial Size Can of Whoop Ass." Old Benny thought that all of us CCPs were going to lie down and cry because they delivered a mighty blow for Allah. The only thing that Benny's group did was show, the world what cowards they are. I put Benny's group in the same category with women/child abusers and cockroaches. Have you ever noticed when you turn on a light the roaches and woman/child abusers run for the cover of darkness? The irony of it all is that we have card-carrying members in the military that are Muslim, looking for Benny and his cronies, and their main objective is to arrange a face-to-face meeting for Benny, his cronies, and Allah. As was stated previously, CCP members are a force to be reckoned with, and Benny and his gang are finding this out first hand. What is that old saying…? "Sucks to be you!"

Who would you say is one of the most famous CCPs in America? Archie Bunker, of course! From the 1950s to the middle of the 90s, this was your typical CCP. Archie had an answer for everything and if he did not have the correct one at that time, he would make one up. Race, religion, politics, food and money - no subject was outside his extensive range of knowledge, but he would dance around the discussion if it concerned sex. Without a doubt, Archie Bunker belongs in the CCP Hall of Fame as a founding member. I am sure that there were some wanna-be CCPs prior to television coming into its heyday and Archie was one of those people sitting around the radio. Since that time was prior to the majority of us "Baby Boomers," this period is not eligible for the Hall of Fame.

With the onset of television in the late 1940s, the "Soap Opera Queen" era was thrust upon the American public. The never ending "Soap Operas" were born. Trivia fact: The reason these shows were called soap operas was due to the fact that the majority of the advertisers were soap companies. And with this new avenue to dream, or escape from the reality of day-to-day housework, the seeds of the original CCPs were planted. In the 50's, 60's and 70's, there was a steady increase in "Soap Operas" and viewers, insomuch as by the mid-70's, soaps were on "Prime Time." How could any self-respecting CCP forget such classics as Dallas, Dynasty, Knot's Landing and a host of other socially redeeming shows? Let's face it, most of us Baby Boomers can remember where we were when JFK was shot, and most of us can remember where we were when we found out who shot J.R. With most of the television stations going off the air at midnight, CCPs got a chance for some sleep, but with the onset of cablevision, sleep became an option. Think about it, television twenty-four hours a day. CCPs had just reached Nirvana. We are not saying these shows from midnight to 6 a.m. had any substance (ESPN was a good example), but then again we are not saying any show from 6 a.m. to midnight had any substance either.

Daytime Programming:

Soap Operas

What exactly is a soap opera? Nothing but one of those trashy romance novels in video format! Let's visit one of these shows while it is in progress: The Town: Hornyville, USA; The Location: Dr's office, Judge's Chambers, the grocery store, and the golf course; The Time: 10:30 am; The Scene: Clothes are flying and bodies are bumping. It looks like a mating frenzy of rabid minks. And this is before noon; wait till' you see the swing shift in action. There is more sex on TV in daytime programming than there ever was in prime time, and the violence starts with the local evening news. Have you noticed that there are not that many fat people on these shows? We have all heard from doctors and others that sex is a great workout and calorie burner and this is living proof. Look at these people, they are screwing so much they don't have time to eat, and the majority of them are anorexic. But most of all these people aren't picky with whom they screw, because there have been shows where they had sex with spirits/demons, aliens (no offense meant for our alien chapter... these are aliens YOU guys wouldn't even touch with a photon torpedo), time travelers and more. There seems to be two requirements regarding sex partners: breathing and a pulse. Now that was a stupid statement since the prior sentence described having sex with sprits, which have neither a pulse nor the ability to breathe. Let's change the requirements to "if the person/sprits/demon/alien or whatever has the correct equipment to have sex." ***SHOWTIME!!***

Where in the real world have you seen a woman cleaning the house in a thousand dollar evening dress, or a man working on his car in a new Armani suit? Only in the soaps! You will never know when the right moment for sex will appear and you have to look your best, don't you? With all of this shameless sex taking place on all of these shows, there is one common factor that no one has picked up on, and now the truth can be told. None of these people are Orthodox Catholics. The reason we know this is due to the fact every square inch of the planet is not covered with a person. Without birth control and abortion, and that much sex taking place, there would not be a piece of dry land that did not have a body on it.

The most amazing thing is that these people have short memories. They give a whole new meaning to the term "out of sight, out of mind." A good example is in the program All My Children. Tad Martin and his brother were ordered upstairs to the attic to get the ski equipment for the upcoming trip. Tad and his brother went upstairs, Tad came down, and no one has seen or heard from the brother in thirty years. Where is Child Protective Services when you need them? The poster child for gold diggers is also on this show... Erica (who knows what her last name is this week). Erica has been married more times than the entire state of Vermont's population and, while she is married, she is humping the next future husband because she knows the present one isn't going to last. Erica is getting nailed so often she can definitely relate to the feelings of a pin-cushion. Susan Lucci, please don't feel so bad about being snubbed in the daytime Emmys all those years. You of all people should know how women are and the rest of the female population was jealous of you and all the action you were getting and you weren't sharing. Keep up the good work, and spread all the love and joy around town.

What is really amazing is that some of these shows have been on TV for over forty years: Days of Our Lives, Edge of Night, General Hospital, etc. That means a good portion of the US politicians was raised on the "Guiding Light" ways of the world. Maybe that is the reason we see all the sex scandals in government. They just can't tell the difference between the real world and Hornyville. Here is an idea for two new daytime shows: 1. As The Senate Yearns; and 2. The Humps and Bumps of the House. (Note for screenwriters: for these shows, material should be easy to come by - CSPAN or the evening news.)

Tabloid Tv

In the 80's a new breed of CCPs arrived on the scene. "Talk Show Junkies." And whom do we have to blame for this phenomena? What one show took our society on a short slippery slope to the gutter? Let's rephrase that, to the sewer? The "Godfather" of tabloid TV... Phil Donahue, that's who, Donahue's show was syndicated in 1974 and it was based in Chicago. The "Windy City," was that apropos or just a Freudian slip? The show stayed in Chicago until 1985 and then it was moved to New York City where it lasted until 1996. Contrary to what some preachers have said, Phil is not the Anti-Christ; maybe one of his demons, but definitely not the Anti-Christ.

Phil was King of the Hill, or thought he was until a lady from Mississippi rode into town. Is that why Phil went to New York and what do I know, I thought Chicago was a big town. The lady's name was Oprah Winfrey. Now she is in that Diva league that does not require a last name, such as Cher, Madonna, and now there is **OPRAH.** Oprah came onto the scene and her show's ratings booted Phil off the hill. She then began to lay the foundation for her empire at the top of that hill. Presently she is sitting rather elegantly on her throne as the "Queen of Everything." You thought I was going to say queen of tabloid TV. Little did you know, this woman is more powerful that Bill Gates, politicians, and a host of wanna-be's. Let's face it. When a powerful late night talk show host whines and grovels about never being invited on her show, you know she has the power. (A note to David

Letterman regarding getting on the show: remember the toes that you step on are connected to the feet that are connected to the ass you will have to kiss to get on the show. In other words, pucker up.) Oprah is presently being investigated. The Federal Government thinks she is a monopoly. After all, the government went after Bill Gates and he isn't into as many industries as Oprah. But courts do not scare the Queen. She kicked the Texas Cattleman Association's butt in a lawsuit, and we all know there was a lot of bull coming out of the courtroom. The lady had taken her show down the sleazy path for a while and then she took control of her own destiny and changed the format. The formats today are informative and entertaining, but remember she is the person that brought us the "Drive-Thru Psycho Psychiatrist" Dr. Phil. We will get even with her one-day for unleashing this new plague on the American public.

The next uplifting and educational program I will talk about is hosted by the Satan of Sleaze himself, Jerry Springer. You know you have just tuned into a show for the whole family when you see Bouncers & Bodyguards on stage while the people are being interviewed. The comedian Jeff Foxworthy has a routine that says, "You know you are a redneck when your family tree has no branches." On that note, if the Springer show could get a group picture of all the people that have been on the show and then did a genealogy drawing of their families, you would have a picture of a forest of telephone poles. Jerry's show was not the first to have violence as part of the mainstay of the program. Who can forget that outstanding show that Geraldo Rivera put on with the White Supremacist and the Jewish panel? Where was the "Politically Correct Police" when you needed them? For that matter, where was the real police when this show was being taped? When the fists and chairs quit flying around on the set, you see a picture of Geraldo with a bandage on his nose looking somber and dazed. Let's take a poll: who do you feel more pity for - Geraldo or the chair that hit him? Here is a hint for Jerry's show, (one that will save the producers money on props and fixtures); bolt the chairs down to the stage.

One question that has always amazed me is why would anyone knowingly go on the Jerry Springer show? I mean, you know your life is in the toilet before you get there, and yet you are going to let all of America see Jerry pull the handle of the toilet and flush you out of your misery? Maybe these people are tricked into going on to the show. Picture this and see if it would work for you. You come home from work and your spouse/partner/sister/brother/transvestite announces you have just won a trip to Chicago. This trip that you won contains travel tickets (could be airline, could be a bus), lodging, meals and front row tickets to the Jerry Springer show. Your first clue that your ass is in a crack would be when they sit you down in a chair and start applying makeup and placing the microphones on your body. To get me in front of the cameras the producers would have to strap me to an M-1 Tank and drag me to that stage and, trust me, it would be a hell of a fight to keep me on that stage. But, hey, that's just me. But let's face it, the majority of the people that go on this show have a common factor, their IQ's are identical to their shoe size. News Flash: On January 24, 2003, Jerry Springer announced that he is going to run for the U.S. Senate. Answer this question if you can... Is Jerry wanting to help the people of Ohio (he is a former mayor of Cincinnati) or, is he just trying to cut down on his expenses? Anyone that has ever watched CSPAN knows you can see some of the same antics on the Senate floor that you have seen on Jerry's stage.

The next show that has just captured America's heart is the Jenny Jones Show. This show's main theme is trying to redress all of the 14 and 15 year-old hookers in America. The Princess of the "Wonder Bra," Jenny has taken it upon herself to get all of the young girls in America to change their way of dress. God forbid that any of them would show up on Mr. Blackwell's worst dressed list. Jenny brings these girls to the show along with their mothers. The girls receive a make over and new clothes, and all is right with the world at the end of the show.

This is definitely a safer show than the ones in the past where one of the participants killed a gay acquaintance/friend a few days after the show. The show theme was "Fantasies/Secret Crushes." This gay guy ends up telling all of America that he has a crush on his friend and, of course, this "Macho" guy could not take the humiliation, and a few days later, murdered the gay man. To me this is the very bottom of entertainment. This program is not in the sewer; it has made it all the way to the wastewater treatment plant.

Then there are the shows that have won an honorable-mentioned prize: Maury, Montel Williams, and Ricki Lake. It seems that Maury's two major themes are 1) is his guest a man or woman 2) DNA testing. It seems he has had one guest on the show looking for the father of her child and, to date, the show has tested six men that she knew their names, the entire audience, and half of Detroit. And we still do not know who the father is. Montel wants to be huggy-feely and have everyone up to that great statement of Rodney King's "Can't we all get along?" With regards to Ricki Lake, who cares?

Court Tv

Here we enter another era of social redeeming rhetoric. One of the first court programs was The People's Court, with kindly old Judge Wapner. The majority of his cases you would find in your local municipal or small claims court. Nothing really earth shattering, sexy, or criminal, just two or three people that could not stand the sight of each other. There would be some yelling or screaming but in the end, the Judge would settle everyone down and hand out his ruling. Once the ruling was announced, both parties would go out into the hallway and talk with some clown from the show, who would be asking them to describe their feelings. Just once, everyone would have loved to see one of the parties grab that microphone and shove it somewhere the announcer definitely would not have wanted it and then ask him how **HE** felt. Talk about getting a rise in the ratings. That would have done it!!

The People's Court is still on the air, but we have some major competition nowadays; Divorce Court, Judge Hatchett, Judge Joe Brown, Judge Judy, Judge Mathis and last but not least *Texas Justice.* Don't you know that last one (Texas Justice) sends shivers up and down the spines of criminals everywhere. Do you realize that if we could get two more court TV shows, we would have as many judges sitting on the bench on TV as in the U.S. Supreme Court? Just think, the judges on TV would be easier to remove than the "Supremes." Cancel the show and then add a new one. After some of the rulings the "Supremes" have made over the past thirty years, you know the minor league judges on TV could do no worse.

OK so we can't allow the TV judges to replace the "Supremes." How about letting them handle real State cases, like assault, robbery, rape, murder and other various felonies. The U.S. Constitution guarantees each defendant a speedy trial... if you can't say that 30 minutes isn't speedy, then I don't know what to say. Can you imagine Judge Judy on the bench for the O.J. Simpson trial and the appellate judge would be that cowboy from *Texas Justice.* Think about it - each state's court dockets are so booked up it takes months, maybe years, for some cases to come to trial, and along with all of the motions and delays, expenses add up. If these cases were seen on TV, the states could save money in their judicial budget;1.) They would not need as many judges and other courtroom personnel, and 2.) Advertisers would pick up the majority of the operating expenses. This is a plausible way of increasing production without increasing expenses and it would be very educational (see chapter 10) for the viewing public. It would bring a whole new meaning to Reality TV and, of course, all Capital Murder trials would go to the "Texas Justice" Court, thus insuring the death sentence would be carried out. You don't think some mamse pamse judge from The People's Court would hand down that extreme sentence, do you?

Prime Time

Horse Operas

Back in time, in that era know as BC (Before Color), there were the "Horse Operas." And the longest running horse opera in television history was GUNSMOKE. Was Marshal Matt Dillon a man's man, or what! He would get on his horse, ride all day chasing the bad guys, catch said bad guys (fight always ensued), ride back into town with bad guys strapped to their horses, and place bad guys in jail under Chester's supervision. And then he would go to the Long Branch Salon to get the dust out of his throat, whereupon meeting his two most trusted friends, Miss Kitty and Doc, and discuss the day's world events. After a night of stimulating conversation and drinking (every night they close the bar down, what else is there to do in that town?), everyone leaves going to their own homes alone and wakes up to a bright shiny world the next day.

Now lets analyze all of the players in this show, starting with Chester. Chester was obviously gay. Let's face it there was nothing wrong with his leg. He had to limp because in that day in age, if he sashayed across main-street, they would have shot his ass. Doc was a junkie, how many times did you see him staring off into space. You have to remember that Cocaine was just coming out as a new miracle drug and no one knew its side effects. Miss Kitty was a hooker and a very successful one at that, she owned the Long Branch Salon. Last, but not least, the Marshal, Dillon, definitely had some serious problems. Miss Kitty was hanging on the Marshal like a cheap suit in every show but did you see him grab her by the hair and drag her up the stairs to one of the bedrooms? No! We all want to believe the morals of TV back in BC were higher, loftier, and cleaner, but now "Enquiring Minds Want To Know." Years later the truth has come out, Dilon suffered from that dreaded disease ED (Erectile Dysfunction). If only he had contacted his U.S. Senator Bob Dole and had a conversation about the wonder drug Viagra, there may not have been so much police violence in Dodge City. Just think, if Marshal Dillon had not been so sexually frustrated or would have had a way to release all of that pent up anger, there would not have been so many occupants in the local "Boot Hill."

Other great classics included Paladon "Have Gun Will Travel", Cheyenne, Wagon Train and the infamous Rawhide. Who can forget its most famous cast member? This manly man, played Rowdy Yates (if that is not a manly name, what is?)! Yes, at the time he was not the silver screen mega star that he is today. But can't you see him off behind some cow practicing his two famous lines, "Go ahead you mangy cattle rustler and make my day," or "You have to ask yourself one question you mangy (you have to remember everyone was mangy in BC) Injun, do you feel lucky?", did he shoot 5 or 6 times? That's right our own truly lovable and always politically correct cop, the one and only Clint Eastwood. Of course we cannot forget Roy Rogers, Gene Autry, Hop Along Cassidy (did they call him HA for short?) and all of the other masters of the saddles.

Here is a deep thought to ponder... one that has come up at several CCP meetings. If there was so much violence on TV in our early years with these cowboy shows (and remember, at any given time in prime time, there were more bullets flying on these shows than were actually in the air in Vietnam) why didn't we "Baby Boomers" take guns to school and shoot up our classmates? Then again, nobody ever said us CCPs were smart. You want proof? You watch the RAW, don't you?

Medical Marvels

Who among you can forget the likes of Ben Casey, Dr. Kildare, or the lovable Marcus Welby MD. All of these shows were definitely before HMOs. Dr. Casey and Kildare had all of the women in America wanting to revert back to their childhood so they could play "doctor" with these two guys. Marcus Welby has gone down in history as the last doctor in America to make a house call. There was not a single disease known to man that these three doctors could not cure. If the Federal Government would quit wasting our tax dollars with groups like the CDC, Cancer research, AIDS research, etc. and send that money to Ben, Kildare, and Marcus, these diseases would have a cure before the summer reruns started. With that said, these programs were basically "Chick Flicks" before there was such a thing, and no true manly CCP would be caught dead watching such programs.

Situation Comedys

Whatever happened to the wholesome shows such as My Three Sons (the 90's version was Roseanne), Leave It To Beaver (Tim Allen's Home Improvement), and that all time favorite Ozzie & Harriet (The Osbournes)? As you can plainly see, the formats haven't changed much, just the actors and actresses. Everyone knows that there is a sitcom playing on TV at this present moment that is a mirror image of your family life and you are just pissed that you are not getting residuals for it. Everyone that watches these comedies wants to escape their mundane life, along with the troubles of the world, if just for a little while. What is that old saying - "Laughter is the best medicine."

The one comedy show that every CCP man dreams about was entitled Gilligan's Island (it should have been called Fantasy Island, but that name was promised to another show). Once again, network executives wanted to make the American public believe that there was no sex taking place on that island. Who are these guys (the executives)?; priests or frustrated Republicans (see chapter 2: Politics regarding frustrated Republicans). Let's take a close look at the castaways. Mr. Thurston Howell, this man was the Bill Gates of his day and don't give me bull that he had his wife with him. Mrs. Howell spent more time being interested in the island's social register and fashion than she did worrying about such trivial things as sex. Then there was the Queen of all "Gold Diggers" Ginger, the movie star. Here was a lifetime opportunity that every gold digger dreams of. Now you do the math, rich old man + old woman + movie star with a body that would make a bulldog fight a bear = $$$$. If Thurston old boy wasn't doing the "ride the wild pony" with Ginger, then shave my legs, wax my body, and use me as a surfboard (I have always wanted to use that line. It is out of the movie "Mummy Returns"). Mary Ann is a different story; the clean wholesome look was all a façade. In reality she was a Dominatrix. You know the type - beat me, hurt me, make me write bad checks. Her suitcase of toys had been lost in the lagoon, but she talked sweetly to Gilligan and convinced him to dive into the lagoon and retrieve it for her. Once her whips and chains were recovered, the beatings began. How, else do you think she could have kept three grown men at her beck and call. Think about it, every time she screamed or shouted they came running. Gilligan must have been her favorite because he always acted like he was punch drunk after having just gone 12 rounds with Mike Tyson.

Reality Tv

Now this is a real oxymoron, Reality TV. Those two words should not be in the same sentence. Maybe being a "Baby Boomer" I do not understand today's meaning of reality as "Generation X" does. Have you ever wondered why they are called "Generation X"? As one very smart lady (my wife) said, "They are so spoiled and they want everything now. Advertisers had to call them something and they could not call them "Generation Assholes" on TV." Unless you are living in a commune or the Playboy Mansion, where in the world are you going to see that many men and women are living together, with all of that backstabbing, lying, screaming, cussing, and sex taking place. Sorry, I forgot to add Congress to the list. I looked up the word "reality" in the dictionary (Riverside Webster's II New College), and nothing I read in the book matched what is being shown on TV. Here are a few of the "Reality TV" shows, and let's look closely at how real they are to the everyday life of the general population.

Survivor

This is the show that takes a group of Generation-Xers and sprinkle in a few Baby Boomers (the Boomers do not have a snow ball's chance in Hell of winning) and drops them off at some barren location on the earth for a month, with the winner getting $1,000,000. Oh, let's not forget that this is also a popularity contest, because this is where the backstabbing, lying, etc. is taking place (maybe this is the training camp for future Congressional personnel). At the end of the show, when it is down to the last two Democrats, (with all of the lying and promises made to get to that position, you know they have to be Democrats) fighting for the million dollars (I rest my case; have you ever seen CSPAN and the Democrats fight for money), it all comes down to a committee vote (enough said) on who was the biggest prostitute. I am sure some of you are upset that I called them prostitutes, but face it, they are selling their bodies and pride for a chance at $1,000,000. Mind you, everyone has their price, and a million dollars is damn close to mine .

Every day in this country we have men training in far worse conditions and their training period is longer than thirty days and there is definitely not a million dollar prize at the end of the rainbow. These men serve in the Army's Rangers & Special Forces, the Marines Recon, and the Navy's SEALs. With the SEALs great history, they also have some bragging rights regarding this show. On the first show, Rudy, an ex-SEAL, was one of the last three contestants. Oh, I forgot to mention Rudy was over 60 years old, and of course all of the contestants from Generation- X/Assholes were constantly making fun of him. But when the dust settled he was fighting to get to the top of the hill when the majority had fallen behind. I guess that old saying is true "Once a Bad Ass, Always a Bad Ass." If Rudy had been twenty years younger, guess who the winner would have been? And it would not have been that overweight exhibitionist, Richard. And the sad part about it? The only thing all of the contestants could agree on was that Richard did not have anything worth exhibiting. If the producers want to show a true survivor program, pit a group of Rangers/SF, Recon, and SEALs against each other and see who gives up first. Just remember this would take a long period of time because these men aren't going to give up easily.

Joe Millionaire

What can I say? Every one of these women are guaranteed to be elected on the first ballot to the "Gold Diggers Hall of Fame." If a family background research was part of the application, we would be sure to find the granddaughter from Ginger and Mr. Howell is on this show. When you go into a U.S. Postal Office, you will still see pictures of wanted felons that the federal law enforcement agencies are looking for. I am proposing that this same technique be installed in every bar in America. And every one of the women that was on this show should have her picture placed upon that board, with the following warning "If you see these women; **_RUN!_** Do not speak to these women! Do not buy these women a drink! If they ask you what type of car you drive tell them it is a 1974 Vega station wagon." Any man in America that would marry any one of these women without a prenuptial agreement should be shot the minute he says "I do", thus ensuring he does not reproduce and infest the gene pool with his dumbass genes. What would it take to get the Surgeon General to issue a warning that these women could be hazardous to your wallets?

Meet My Folks

There are two versions of this show, the first being that a female has all of these men to pick from and the second has a guy with all the women that his parents have to sort through. In the first one, the female's parents are asking questions to the men while they are hooked up to a lie detector. The stupidest question that has ever been asked in the history of television was asked by the female's father, **"Are you going to try to have sex with my daughter"**? She is breathing and has a pulse doesn't she? You're damn skippy he is going to try and if he is lucky, he is going to bang her like a screen door in a hurricane. Where was this father's brain when he asked that asinine question? Does he really think these guys are going to tell the truth? This father must have had the first stages of Alzheimer's, because he forgot what it was like to be that age. The truth be known, this man that asked that dumb question was the type of man that women warn their daughters about. Let's face it men, it is a known fact you cannot think with your head and cranium at the same time. I mean, it is an either/or situation - the blood is either in the head or it is being pumped to the cranium. There is scientific proof the male body could not hold the amount of blood to operate the head and cranium at the same time. In other words, the father knew the answer to the question before he asked it. He should have asked a question that plays out in every day life, "Once you marry my daughter and have kids and then divorce her, are you going to pay child support willingly or am I going to have to hunt you down?"

The other show where the parents follow the same format with the lie detector ask the same questions but this time the questions are being asked to the women. But the same questions are not as stupid. Why you ask, because the son and father got together before the show and planned the questions. This way the father is helping his son not waste his time and the son will have a list of sure bets. Of course the mother is not too crazy about this idea, but what the heck, it's a man thing, right? News Flash: One of the contestants has been labeled a "Soft Porn Queen." It seems she has done several movies and her specialty is "Tickle Fetish." You can bet your sweet butt old Dad is going to use an industrial size highlight marker on that name when he gives the son the list. This show may be the closest to the real world as any of them that are being shown. All of us have had to meet the parents at one time or another, but truthfully I do not know very many people that have been hooked up to a lie detector (although a good majority should have been).

There have been several other reality shows that will endure the test of time, such as **WHO WANTS TO MARRY A MILLIONAIRE?**   Now here is a genuine classic, the "millionaire" was a true winner and this was his last chance to get laid (he failed) and the blonde bimbo that "won" did not know what she was getting into.   Did she truly believe that all of us CCPs are as dumb as she is and, remember she wasn't doing this for the "money"?   Or, was that the statement she made after the spread for Playboy?   Remember the "Gold Diggers Hall of Fame" posters in the bars across America?   All the female participants of this show should have their pictures added to the board as well.

The Bachelorette

This is nothing but a rejected, pissed off woman, remember she was a reject from The Bachelor, and these so-called men are going to try to woo her affection.   Have these guys ever heard that old saying, "Hell hath no fury like a woman scorned"?   These guys are thinking, "Hot babe, hot tub" and she is thinking, "If I get hold of the family jewels I am going to hang them up in my trophy room."   Have you ever noticed when she sends one or two guys packing from the show she is whistling a little tune?   I have got it from good sources the tune is one of Queen's classics "Another One Bite The Dust."   To all of the female CCPs reading this book, stay away from these men; obviously these are not true men.   What true man would go on nationwide TV to get spanked and humiliated, and then, at the end, act as if it were no big deal to be rejected?   Trust me ladies, you do not want to be seen with any of these mama's boys unless they have spent a few weeks with Mary Ann on Gilligan's Island.

And then you have **FEAR FACTOR**, and what is this show?   It is basically the poor man's version of Survivor.   The production company saves money on finding contestants by digging through the dumpster from the Survivor's offices. These people are showing the American public what they are willing to do for $50,000 (none of the Einsteins realizes that the IRS is going to get a good portion). Remember what was said earlier, that everyone has a price. Well these people's price is in the "After the fire & water damage sale" range.

This was just a little background in the history of television programs. Yes, I could have written a paragraph on every show but the first chapter would have been as many pages as the Bible so you basically got a "Reader's Digest" version. In upcoming books, I will give you more insight to television history. What everyone has to realize is that, to be a card carrying CCP does not mean the addiction is only to the television. We are now in the 21st Century and that means computers and wireless communication.

21st Century Communication

Evolution Of Communication

How did the world ever rotate around it's axis before the epidemic of computers was unleashed on the general public? Trust me, I am not against computers; I am writing this book on a computer. If the truth was known as to how atrocious my spelling is (thank God for a spell checker), the liquid paper or correct-a-tape companies would get a law passed through Congress requiring me to use a typewriter, thus ensuring that their stocks would show a steady (if not out of sight) increase. I am one of those rare individuals that look at a computer as a tool, not my only source to the outside world (and I mean the planet earth), or my escape from reality, or source of sexual pleasure. I know some computer fanatics that debate "The Power of the Computer" and some of these people have truly felt the power, by sticking their hand in the back of the monitor while it was running. Take a trip down the new wing of CCP's Headquarters and visit with the PC/Wireless Communication card carrying CCPs (majority card holders are members of Generation-X [my daughter told me I could not use "Asshole" anymore, since she is in this group]). The evolution of wireless communication starts with PCs, then evolves into cell phones, and now we are into PDAs/Blackberries.

Personal Computers

On July 29, 1969, an onboard computer was attempting to land the Eagle on the moon. Neil Armstrong and Buzz Aldrin were basically there for the ride and secondary backup for the computer. No one has ever answered this question... When the computer crashed, did the dreaded blue screen appear? Yes, the computer failed, and Neil Armstrong had to manually fly the craft down for a safe landing. To show you the evolution of computers and how far we have come, here is a comparison. The computer that was onboard the Eagle would not be powerful enough to run a modern day "Game Boy" that your kids play with in the back seat of the car (this alone is the true cause of road rage).

Have you ever noticed the conspiracy that is taking place in this country with regard to computer manufacturers? And our government is not doing a damn thing about it because they are also making money off of it through taxes. The conspiracy that I am talking about deals with the speed in which new equipment is put on the market. Remember when all the rage was the "286 processor"? Next came the Pentium (I am back; I had to get on my hands and knees to look at my computer to see how to spell Pentium), then Pentium II, Pentium III, and now Pentium IV. This evolution in hardware is not the source of my anger. This is just the natural order of things, is it not?

What really ticks me off is these new products come out just as soon as you sent your last payment in and now the product is yours and it is a frigging dinosaur. Of course you cannot keep the old computer. Your kids would be psychologically scarred for life if their friends knew they were having to work on such a slow computer. Modern day kids would rather be seen in the back seat of your 1975 AMC Gremlin than have their friends know that their family is out of step with the cyber world. And least we forget if your computer has a 56K modem and not a DSL line, Child Protection Services has a file on you for severe mental anguish.   For all of you Baby Boomers, have you ever noticed that when you ask one of the members of Generation-X to help you, or explain something new on the computer, you get that little smirk that translates into "You dinosaur"? The next time you get that look, take a deep breath, look the youngster in the eye and say, "I can do math without a calculator, can you?" Then walk away whistling Queen's tune "We are the Champions."

Microsoft. Doesn't that word send shivers up and down the spine of every computer literate person in the world? The Federal Government went after the big "M" and the only reason this happened was due to the fact the other software makers were mad that they did not think of the big "M's" tactics first. The monopoly lawsuit does not effect the every day CCP because our machines will have "Windows." Most of our CCPs could not name three other software makers and who cares if it did not come loaded on my machine, the higher form of life in the evolution of computers deems it unworthy of my household, and thus, that is the reason "Windows" is on our machines. Microsoft is just as crafty as the hardware makers in the evolution of their products, with the exception that we (CCPs), the end users, are the testing department. Haven't you noticed that, first there was Windows, then Windows 95, Windows 98, Windows 2000, and now, Windows XP? The bad part about this marketing scheme is when Microsoft finally works out all of the bugs in their software and things are working the way they should have from the first day you purchase it, Whamo, another convention in Las Vegas and the new product hits your computers and the testing starts all over again. There are laws on the books to protect our citizens from certain addiction (cocaine, meth, heroin, etc.) but no one has looked into the software addiction. Mr. Bill Gates is the envy of the business world for what he and his partners have developed. But whether Mr. Gates or Mr. Paul Allen will admit it, they are card-carrying CCPs. How many hours do you think these men have spent looking at a computer monitor?

E-Mail

This has cost every man, woman, and child part of the families' annual income and this includes people that do not even have an e-mail address. How can this be? One-word: competition. The U.S. Postal Service (or known in the cyber world as "snail mail") is losing money every year to e-mail. Did you know that it is in the U.S. Constitution that businesses are required to use the Post Office for the majority of their mail? But since e-mail can be sent without the company paying another courier service, this law is not valid. So the U.S. Mail is getting less and less letters and packages sent through their systems, which means the Post Offices are showing a yearly loss, and this now becomes the justification for a postal rate increase. Of course, no one in the government has the insight to look at a simple law of business (which every graduate of any business school learned in Business 101), "If overhead and/or expenses are greater than income reduce the first two." But this is another subject that will be covered in Chapter 2.

There is no doubt that e-mail has revolutionized the world of communication, there is no waiting three or four days for a response. Do you realize how many jokes and cartoons are flying around on the information highway at this very moment? And some office manager or some other boss (that is kissing his/her way up the corporate ladder) has made it their mission in life to keep said jokes/cartoons out of their offices. Loss of productivity, you know. I guess they never heard that old saying "Laughter is the best medicine." And with the state of the economy these days, you need something to laugh at because most business profits (or lack thereof) would make anyone cry. A manager would have a better chance winning the Lotto than stopping the jokes and cartoons from coming into the office. I am a die-hard fan of all of the jokes and cartoons I receive from my friends. This is the way I start my day with a laugh, and then usually it is downhill from there. E-mail has spawned other enterprises that have kept our male CCPs out of the doghouse, such as the e-mail card industry. You can send Valentine cards, Birthday cards, sexy cards, kinky cards and the ever I-am-so-sorry-it-will-never-happen-again-I-am-lower-than-whale-doo-doo card (of course the female CCP members never need the latter card).

The next rung up the electronic food chain is the "CHAT ROOM." There are chat rooms ranging from Aliens (no offense intended to our alien chapter) to Zebra mating habits. If there is a subject matter that you need help with, trust me, there is a chat room out there willing to pull you in, basically in the same manner as a black hole would do with a nearby star. There have been reported cases of people entering chat rooms and never being seen or heard from again.   Kind of reminds you of episodes from The Outer Limits or The Twilight Zone, doesn't it? Maybe these shows were ahead of their time. Just on a slim chance there is not a chat room regarding your particular subject, it is obvious it is not worth discussing. There was a common factor that held the PC, e-mail and the dreaded chat room together and that was the telephone line or DSL line, but as Darwin stated in his Thesis of Man, or whatever it was called, evolution is forever evolving, thus we move into the wireless communication era of man/woman. See, I am trying to evolve into a modern PC man (sorry about that); old habits are hard to break - PC *Person*.

Cellphones

This instrument is truly one of the curses that Moses inflicted upon Egypt: it just arrived 4,000 years too late. These royal pains in the ass give a whole new meaning to that old AT&T commercial, "Reach out and touch someone." Why is it that if you make a connection to your favorite girl/boy/parent/ alien/whatever on the other side of the planet (especially when you are in a restaurant), you have to talk loud enough for them to hear you without using the phone? How many times have you been in a public restroom, washing your hands or whatever, and you hear a cell-phone go off in one of the stalls and then, to top it off, the idiot answers the phone! How many times have you been driving down the freeway and see a person on the cell phone in one hand carrying on a very heated conversation and, to make matters worse, this clown is one of those people that has to talk with their hands? I want to know what is steering the car. If the occupant in the car is a member of our alien chapter, I can understand that (extra appendages are standard equipment), but if they are your every day run of the mill human, what the hell is steering the car?

For the majority of the people that own a cell phone, this is a dangerous tool and it is high time that states issue licenses in the same manner as they would a driver's license. The test would involve a written portion along with a test call section.

Written section could look like the following:

True or False:

1. Have been off the phone long enough in the past 12 hrs to eat.
2. Have been off the phone long enough in the past 12 hrs to sleep.
3. Have been off the phone long enough in the past 12 hrs to bathe.
4. You are more worried about your supply of phone batteries than your 401K.
5. Your idea of a long meaningful relationship includes unlimited minutes.

The test-call section would something like this;

1. Visual inspection of the equipment. Note: If you have had the phone surgically implanted to your ear, you just failed.
2. Can you walk and breathe at the same time?
3. Do you look for the speed dial button to start your car?

For all of you cell phone CCPs, just remember that if you are involved in a car accident while talking on the phone, you will lose your CCP card. The only way to get your card reinstated would be to attend a CCP certified Driving/Phone School. In these classes you will be required to watch 40 hours of the Jerry Springer show and 40 hours of Dr. Phil. If you come out of this school and are not in a catatonic state your card will be reinstated. Just remember you went through Dante's first stage of Hell. And, if you have another accident, you don't even want to know what Dante's second ring looks like. As a matter of fact, the law will not allow us to tell you what programs that you would be required to watch; and you know there are some bad ones out there, such as "My Mother the Car".

Not only can you talk on your cell phone, now it can take pictures, receive e-mails, stock updates, walk the dog, fix dinner and pick winning lotto numbers for you. Why would you ever want to leave home when you have an instrument that can do everything for you? Oh, and let's not forget, check your bank balance for the direct deposit of your paycheck, assuming you have done something in all that time to justify you getting paid.

P.D.A./Blackberry

If you do not know what a PDA/Blackberry is, just skip to chapter 2 because to bring you up to speed on these modern wonders would truly make you feel like a dinosaur. The PDA started out as a replacement for your little black book, then it replaced the three ring binders known as the Day Timer. This new fangled tool does everything with the exception of changing the oil in your car. Not only do you have at your fingertips all the telephone numbers in the world and your schedule until the next millennium, you can receive anyone else's information that they want to send you by wireless communication. These machines have games, maps, e-mail, and can send you that very important and timely message to sell all of your Enron stock. These machines are starting to look more and more like Dr. McCoy's Medical Tricorder on the original Star Trek. Look into the future, you call your doctor (on the PDA/Blackberry because they are phone-capable now) and he gives you a complete physical through the PDA/Blackberry. He tells you to place the instrument on your bicep so he can check your blood pressure, next he instructs you to hold it to your forehead to check your temperature. But I will draw the line when he instructs me to use it for a prostate exam.

2.   POLITICS

"I believe a self-righteous liberal or a radical conservative with a cause is more dangerous than a Hell's Angel with an attitude." ... *Anonymous*

History

In 1968, I was a kid in high school and I attended my first political rally in Pensacola, Florida. I do not recall the exact date, but I do remember a few things 1: It was held at the airport (short speech - P'cola was not that big of a town), 2: It was a candidate for the office of the President, 3: He was an independent candidate that was seriously challenging the two major parties. But the most important thing I remember was that a majority of the people across the country thought that this person was a clown, a buffoon, and other not so nice descriptions, but he had people at that time thinking "outside the box." And please don't assume that I agree with his way of life, but I do agree with this one statement, "If you poured all of the Democrats and Republicans into one bag and then shook the bag up, then you poured them out all you would see that there is not a nickel's difference between them." George Wallace. In this day and age and factoring in inflation, you can up the amount to a dollar.

Politics

That word alone gets more reaction out of people than any other word in the English language (making English the required language in the U.S. alone can create its own fire storm). The first thing most people do when a politician walks into the room is to grab their wallets or their asses because they know they are about to be screwed. The majority of CCPs would rather have a root canal without any pain killers than sit through another season of TV ads for political campaigns. At the end of the night after watching three to four hours of campaigns in "Prime Time" TV, with all the mud that has been slung by both sides in the race, if you do not feel dirty, then you are either a mud wrestler or all the nerve endings in your body have short circuited.

The first televised State of the Union address was given by Harry Truman in 1947, and that was basically all of the political coverage TV played until the 1960 elections. The power of television won the Democrats the office in the White House that year. This was the first live televised debate between two Presidential candidates, John Kennedy and Richard Nixon. John Kennedy came to the television station and allowed the make-up artist to apply their trade and then he proceeded to go on stage looking as if he stepped off the cover of GQ magazine. Richard Nixon, on the other hand, came to the station refusing the make-up (unmanly), walked on stage, and when the lights came on he looked like death eating a cracker. The 1960 Presidential election was the closest in U.S. history (that was until the State of Florida hung someone named Chad and elected George W) and many historians say the reason

Nixon lost the election was due to the television debate. Not only did Nixon's appearance have a major impact on the votes, but his style of debate (or lack thereof) failed to sway many voters. This one TV program spawned a new political arm and this new industry would turn into a powerful machine. Today, every politician lives for his or her sound bite to make the national news and, what they don't realize is the majority of the CCPs looks at these sound bites and then screams, "Bite Me".

The next major political statement that was made on TV was during the 1964 Presidential election between Lyndon B. Johnson and Barry Goldwater. The night before the election, an ad ran on all three major networks (yes youngsters, this was before cable and satellite TV). The scene begins with a little girl sitting in a field of flowers and all of a sudden in the background a nuclear explosion goes off and you then see the mushroom cloud. The message? Elect Goldwater and he will lead America into a global nuclear war. The ad worked and Johnson was elected, in the largest landslide in America's history. This just reinforced the political machines as to the power of television.

"Fuzzy Math"

The power of television regarding political campaigns is mind numbing (then again a lot of the CCPs don't have much of a mind to numb) and the happiest people of all are the network executives. The millions of dollars that are spent for political ads during a major election could run several small countries for a couple of years and is definitely higher than Afghanistan's GNP. Would someone please explain to me the rationality of running for a public office such as U.S. Senator and personally spending ten to twenty million dollars for a job that pays $150,000 a year? Let's face it... These are not dumb people (for the most part) or they would not have that kind of money to spend so freely. I was taught in college that you always want a short time period to recover your investment/out of pocket expenses. A term in the senate is six years, 6 x $150K = $20,000,000. I confess I had to go to summer school in 8th grade because I flunked "New Math" during the regular session, but some how I do not know any type of math (true I have not mastered "Fuzzy Math") that will make this equation come true. And you truly expect all of us to believe that line of bull - "Deep down in her/his (how about that PC police!) heart, the idea of being a public servant is their idea of giving back something to this great country that has been so generous to them and their families." And if you believe that, I was the Valet parking attendant on the moon that took care of the moon rover while the astronauts went exploring. Getting back to the numbers, do they teach these future politicians a new form of physics that teaches you how to have your investments jump to warp speed while they (politicians) remain on earth, kissing babies (we are not talking about interns), acting as the person next door, the savior of Social Security & Medicare. I know that a whole lot of our CCP members are smarter than me, and if they can compute this math or can show me the true equation, please forward it to me. I am always looking to expand my horizons (and my bank account).

There are two rules for when a politician is lying 1.) she/he is breathing, 2.)her/his lips are moving. Here are two of the most famous (walk around the truths) recorded statements to ever come out of the White House; 1.) George Bush Sr. "Read my lips (this should have been a clue, rule #2) no new taxes," 2.) Bill Clinton "I did not have sex with that woman." All of us CCPs are very interested in both of those subject matters, (money & sex), and it seems we are particularly interested in money more than sex because George did not get re-elected, but then again, maybe the only reason Bill got re-elected was that the public wanted to see if there was more to come regarding the Oval Office Olympics. In the next book I will have another chapter regarding politics and politicians because there is so much information out there. Who knows - maybe one day there will be a book dedicated to these public servants. If any of you card carrying CCPs have any information on these easy targets of enjoyment (I mean public servants) and you want to share it with the world, please feel free to forward material to me. You know God has to have a sense of humor, he created politicians for us to enjoy, didn't he?

Laws That Govern Most Of The Land

Here is a tid bit of information that the majority of the CCPs do not know. When our public servants are sitting in the lap of luxury, sorry, I meant the hallowed halls of Congress, and passing all of these laws that govern our great nation, there is a special group that does not have to obey these laws. And who is that special group that is excluded from these laws? The Federal Government, that's who! Minor laws such as, America Disability Act (ADA), OSHA, EEOC, Sexual Harassment, and Age Discrimination, are just a few laws that do not apply to them. Remember that old saying "Do as I say, not as I do" (alright so I modified it a bit). Here is a good example of the Feds doing as they wish. In light of the space shuttle disaster (Columbia), news of a massive firing of a panel of experts overseeing the safety of the space program came to light in a press conference. Six months prior to the disaster, this panel gave Congress a report stating that within three or four shuttle launches a major disaster could occur and the main reasons that this could take place was due to budget cuts and cost savings in maintenance. The director of NASA fired six of the panel members and said in a press conference on Television that these six members were fired not for the report that was given to Congress, but they have been on the panel too long and he needed young people with fresh ideas to guide NASA in the future. Can you imagine what would have happened if any company in America would have even thought that, much less SAID it out loud and God forbid if it was whispered at a press conference. This would be a good news/bad news situation. Good news for the airline industry. It will have every seat filled with federal agencies employees (JOD, FBI, DOC, DOT, XYZ, etc., etc.), thus ensuring their profits are soaring so we will not have to bail them (airlines) out again. And let's not forget all of the private lawyers that will be circling the fresh Feds kill waiting to get at the remainder of the carcass. The bad news is the Feds' will be at the company's headquarters before the news conference would be over. Does anyone know what the view looks like from atop of Mt. Olympus? Surely this must be the place our leaders live because it sure isn't the real world where us mere mortals reside.

"I know what sex is and there are not varying degrees of it. If I received sex from one of my subordinates in my office, it wouldn't be a private matter or my personal business. I would be FIRED immediately!" This true statement was sent to me via e-mail and I do not know who the author is but I agree with the statement. The other law that the elite politicians do not have to obey deals with sexual harassment or, simply put, screwing your employees (literally this time, most of the time, it is figuratively). Before the Congressman (I can say man this time because this one is a male) from California had an intern come up missing (and I believe him when he said it was not a long meaningful relationship), it was perfectly legal to date, have sex with or not have sex with (White House version), play like Mary Ann (Gilligan's Island) with anyone on their staff. Prior to this law being passed, said staff members basically did not have any recourse for the actions directed at them unless they moved on to another job. But since that intern came up missing, Congress passed a law that states no member of Congress can "Date/Relationship" any member of their staff. Why did they waste time and money by passing a new law, just use the ones that are already on the books. With this new law, all that happens is that you make your colleague's interns fair game, now the politicians can sample different parts of the country and never leave their offices. By the way, to find this law, go to the Dept. of Interior, then go to the Dept. of Fish & Wildlife and look up the hunting regulations. I have not looked up the law personally, but surely there is a bed (I meant bag) limit to the number of interns that can be mounted on their trophy walls per year. Passing this ridiculous law and allowing congress to prey on others staff ranks right up there as making a convicted rapist a gynecologist. The real reason Congress was not about to use the laws already on the books is very simple. If they use one, then every law would apply to them and they are not about to let this happen.

It's hilarious how short the memory of these politicians are, if it were not for costing all of us CCPs to dig deeper in our purses and wallets. Example 1996: "Contract With America" (especially regarding term limits). All the Republicans made a big showing and party at the signing of this document. It is now 2003 and my question is how many of the people that signed that contract lived up to the part regarding term limits? Here is another silly question, if one Democrat had signed that document would it have become a binding agreement? Wouldn't that have opened a can of worms? Is it true that one of the songs that are not allowed to be played in the Capital Building is that great Temptation's song "Ball of Confusion?" Do you remember when the Republicans were screaming for "Campaign Reform" when the Clinton administration was renting out the "Lincoln Room" as if it were a Motel 6 (the DNC did drop the campaign slogan "We'll keep the light on")? But the minute the elephants started guarding the halls of power, they cannot even spell campaign reform must less try to pass a reasonable bill. Please do not think I am picking on the Republicans because the Democrats are just as self-centered and self-serving. Remember when the "Jackasses" (or is that a donkey) were in power before the contract signers and there was not a single sheet of campaign reform to help prevent the Lobbyist from running the country. These reforms are designed to keep such fine upstanding organizations in line and make it fair for all the little boys and girls to play together in the sand box.

Lobbyists help our elected officials to see the error of their ways if they are not voting for their lobbyists' legislation. Lobbyists will create, prepare, educate, and finance any piece of legislation that their organization believes the country cannot live without. Neil Cavudo of the Fox News Channel made a very interesting statement regarding political contributions and that statement was, "Money is the mother's milk of politics"[1]. And, trust me, if that fountain runs dry, you would see most of these politicians on late night infomercials telling you how to invest your money so that you could become an instant millionaire and live the life style you so desperately desire. When was the last time a no-name candidate without lobby backing won an election? I have a great idea for a bloodless coup d'etat. What if every card-carrying CCP registered to vote refused to vote for an incumbent in the next election? Settle down, I can hear the screaming from here. Now the Republicans will have an advantage over the Democrats or vice versa. Each party has to have a primary, correct? Vote the incumbent out in the primary and then when the main election comes up Bingo! a whole new crew of future millionaires. And, by electing new public servants, we will be amazed at how fast the economy

---

[1]   Fox News Channel "Your World", <u>Neil Cavudo</u>, June 17, 2003.

gets out of the red. The lobbyists will have to be spending so much money to ensure they are on the correct bandwagon, thus creating twice as many jobs than prior elections and, who cares who wins the election? Some of that money will eventually trickle down to us peons. Boy wouldn't that scare the hell out of every politician and maybe, just maybe,(I am not promising anything), the politicians may work for the people who voted them into office and not for the lobbyist that pays for all of their good times. Hold on here; I just had a brain fart. Maybe this is one of the components to the equation mentioned above in the paragraph regarding salary and pay back of investment. Maybe the equation should now look like this: 6 x $150,000 x Lobbyist = $20,000,000, but then again what the hell do I know.

How many times have you been watching a political convention, or television show such as "This Week in Congress", "Cross Roads", "Moneyline", Fred & Barney, or whatever, and the main topic is "Fair Share Of The Pie." Along with the discussion, the program has all of these charts and pictures of these pies, but they never tell you what flavor they are, but one thing that is certain is that Jane/John Middle Class Public is paying for this pie. Bear with me and let me see if my simple mind can comprehend this concept. The Republicans own the bakery and they receive the money for the pie. In turn, the Democrats cut up the pie, making sure all of the poor and downtrodden get their fair share (meaning the entire pie), and we (middle class) get the remainder: the pan and the cardboard box. And if we do not recycle these two items, we will be labeled enemies of the planet. With a two-party system in place, the middle class does not have a chance. The Republicans represent big companies and big money and yet they claim they are the true middle class. How many members of the middle class have you ever seen at a Republican fundraiser that did not have to take a second mortgage on their home just to pay for parking and the cover charge? If they want to eat they would have to sell their first born. And the Democrats represent the poor, sick, misbehaving, why did this happen to me group. Go to a Democrat fundraiser. Hell, sometimes you don't have to go anywhere (remember the "Telethons" the party used to hold after the Jerry Lewis big one). They hold auctions, car washes, or promise to hold demonstrations in front of your home unless you pay up. But who represents the true middle class? No one until now!

Third Party

Brothers and Sisters arise. Help is on the way. The middle class now has its' own champion in the political arena, the **CCPP**. The Certified Couch Potato Party is here to protect all of its members, regardless of race, religion, sex, and all of those other fancy descriptions. And our political symbol or mascot (I'm not sure what they call them) is not going to be loud smelly animal that releases hot air from both ends. No, it will be the true symbol that holds all houses and buildings together - Screws and Nails. Why would we use such symbols? What else represents the smorgasbord of America's middle class and the actions that have been done to them in the past? Here is the breakdown of the symbols: The Slotted Screw represents the white CCP members, the slotted screw is the primary screws used by the public and the Democrats have screwed this portion of the middle class for years. The Phillip Head Screw will represent the black and other minority members. Since the Republicans have put the screws to this group they should have their own symbol. And last but not least the Nail will represent the Asians, because both parties have hammered this group since the beginning of time (or at least the 1800's). With as many card carrying members that we have, we will be a force to be reckoned with, and the power of money makes things happen and we are the group that pays for everything the federal government spends. I have a saying in my company and it is "If I am paying, I am telling, but if you are paying, you're telling" and guess what - we have been paying for years.

If we could rename the two major parties and use movie titles, think about the possibilities. My personal favorite for the Republicans is "Grumpy Old Men" and for the Democrats, it would have to be "Animal House." Think back to all of the committee meetings you have seen in the news or on CSPAN and all you see on the Republican side is a bunch of old white guys that have a permanent frown. But you have to admit some of them are now smiling. Is it possible that their buddy Bob Dole has been giving out free samples of the product he advertises for (Viagra)? Who knows? There may be hope and these guys can lighten up some. Can you see it now? Fridays will become Casual Day. Trent Lott is giving a speech on a Friday wearing an Aloha shirt with a pair of "Big Dog" shorts and a wind blown look in his hair. You know, the government may be right; they may need to protect the public from certain things, as the public is not ready for some things, like the fact that there are aliens (we already know that they are here amongst us). But, I am not sure the public is ready for sight of Trent just "hangin'" with the boys. And you have to give it to the Democrats they sure know how to make the word "Party" become a verb instead of a noun. This group has had their fair share of candidates caught with their pants around their ankles. This group really endorses that old slogan "Make Love Not War" but don't you think it is a little tacky when they put their e-mail address at the bottom of that statement, lining up appointments?

Here is another unique idea, every state has to send one Republican and one Democrat Senator to Washington, and the same goes with the House so no one group has the majority. Now comes the fun part, each state would purchase one house for both Senators to live in while Congress is in session and a dorm for the House members. This would make each side see the others point of view. Along with teaching the Republicans how to let down their hair (lets rephrase that: most of them do not have much hair), have a good time (Democrats standards) and the Democrats could learn how to make the money that they are constantly trying to give away. It could happen. Americans walked on the moon, so this should not be that big of a problem. (Note: I am back to reality. My wife made me take my medication so I would not have any more hallucinations.)

Iraqi War

As I sit here contemplating the world and all of its madness I am watching the U.S. slip closer and closer to war (Note this chapter was written in January of 2003). Whether you believe we are going to rid Iraq of an evil leader and his deadly weapons, or you believe George W. and his oil men are going after some choice real-estate, one thing is for sure: It is going to cost money and a lot of it. It has been stated in several news broadcasts that a war will cost $200 **billion,** not mentioning the amount of lives it will cost on both sides. As I stated earlier, I am not the smartest man in the world. My ex-wives and several hundred other people will verify that statement. Here is an old country boy's thought on the subject. Everyone has heard that old saying "Money can buy anything." Well, let's make it work for us. Let's buy a war and not participate and here is how we do it. Looking up the population of Iraq on the internet, it gave me a figure of 23,332,000. Of that 23 million 20% are Kurds (which are on our side) so that leaves us with 18,665,600 Iraqis. Out of this number lets' say 5 million are truly loyal to Saddam. That leaves us with 13,665,600 on our side (our side because we are going to buy them off). If an American soldier or sailor is killed during the war, the government pays to their beneficiary a lump sum amount of $10,000. What if the Allies (if there are any) offer to pay each of the 13,665,600 Iraqis $10,000 to over throw Saddam? That comes to a total of $136,656,000,000, and, to give them a good chance to win, we throw in $14 billion worth of weapons. That brings the grand total up to a $150 billion. We save $50 billion and no U.S. lives are lost. I know all of you think I am not sensitive to the Iraqis that would be fighting, but I am. How many of those people live in poverty? 10,000 U.S. dollars would be more money that they would earn in two lifetimes and with the change of government, their lifestyles could change to that of their neighbors, Saudi Arabia and Kuwait. These two countries share the wealth of the oil fields with their citizens. All of the poor people in the country are imported from other countries to do the every day labor. So there is my version of "What if they gave a war and no one came" (**VERY IMPORTANT NOTE:** as of June 2006, the US has spent **$480 Billion** on the war). If this works here, let's try it in Israel next.

Famous People's Views On Politics

I know what all of you are thinking; that I am prejudice toward politicians. Well I am not. Let's face it; these people do these idiotic stunts of their own free will. And the evening news (chapter 4 covers these yahoos) spends the majority of the show reporting the actions of our esteemed elected officials. Just to prove I am putting a "spin" regarding politics and politicians, just read the following statements that were written as far back as 430 B.C.:

1. A liberal is someone who feels a great debt to his fellow man, which debt he proposes to pay off with your money. – G. Gordon Liddy
2. A government which robs Peter to pay Paul can

always depend on the support of Paul. – George Bernard Shaw

3. Foreign aid might be defined as a transfer from poor people in rich countries to rich people in poor countries. – Douglas Casey (1992)

4. Giving money and power to government is like giving whiskey and car keys to teenage boys. – P. J. O'Rourke

5. Government is the great fiction, through which everybody endeavors to live at the expense of everybody else. – Frederic Bastiat

6. Government's view of the economy could be summed up in a few short phrases: If it moves, tax it. If it keeps moving, regulate it. And if it stops moving, subsidize it. – President Ronald Reagan (1986)

7. I don't make jokes. I just watch the government and report the Facts. – Will Rogers

8. Just because you do not take an interest in politics doesn't mean politics won't take an interest in you. – Pericles (430 B.C.)

9. No man's life, liberty, or property is safe while the legislature is in session. – Mark Twain (1866)

10. Suppose you were an idiot. And suppose you were a member of Congress. But I repeated myself. – Mark Twain

11. The only difference between a taxman and a taxidermist is that the taxidermist leaves the skin. – Mark Twain

12. **What this country needs are more unemployed politicians.** – Edward Langley (this is my personal favorite and it sounds like a great campaign slogan for the CCCP, don't you think?

Why is it you can never get a straight answer out of a politician even if it is a simple one? Example: Reporter "Senator what is you favorite color?" The Senator then states without pausing "Plaid and/or what color would you like it to be?" One of the best examples of this comes from Senator Tom Daschle. In a recent speech, he bomb-blasted President Bush for his way of handling the situation in Iraq. The Senator stated there was no reason for the US to go to war and President Bush had blown the diplomatic chances for a peaceful solution, but when it came time to vote on whether on not to give the President the right to use forces in Iraq, guess which way he voted? The vote was 99 to 0 in favor of war and one Senator was absent due to a family illness. Senator Daschle was not the Senator that missed that vote.

Do these clowns actually think that our memories are so short that we will forget what they promised on Monday, and by Saturday's evening news, we are actually believing the new B.S. spin? Living in a farming community, I know how many headaches the EPA gives the dairy farmers for all of the cow manure and BS their herds produce (it has been reported that the cow population is the major contributor for methane gas in the atmosphere). Obviously the EPA has never done a study in the District of Columbia. Everyone in the country is looking for an alternative source of energy that is not dependant on oil. Here is an idea, and maybe someone can patent it: What if the Capital Building adds a 48" diameter pipe from the dome and runs it to the closest power plant? With all the hot air and methane generated from both houses, it would produce an unlimited supply of fuel, at least while both houses are in session. With all of the hot air and methane generated from the Capital Building, the city, along with the states of Maryland and Virginia would have enough power to reduce everyone's power bill by 95%. And this process would not be limited to the Federal Capital Building. There are fifty states and each one has it own supply of BS in their state capital buildings. I have always wondered; in Moslem countries, whenever a bill comes up in their legislature and a representative/senator adds something to it, do they call it "Beef Barrel Politics" since they will not handle pork?

Enron & Worldcom

Remember when all of the politicians were jumping on this band wagon to help the poor little people that lost their savings/retirement/life savings? All of those big bad executives that took the money were going to feel the wrath of the federal government. New laws were going to be passed to insure that this will not happen in the future. Where are the laws that were promised? Has one gotten out of committee? Why is it the only CEO that is in the process of going to prison is Samuel Waksal? And, what the hell does he have to do with Enron or WorldCom? Nothing; that's what! Sam was the CEO involved with the Martha Stewart scandal and more than likely did not give enough money to the politicians to keep his behind out of the place where everyone wears the same outfit. Armani suits are definitely not the uniform of the day at a Federal Prison Camp. (Again, this is June of 2006 and here is a scoreboard update. Tyco CEO and some underlings have be convicted and heading to a "Club Fed". Enron execs Kenny and whatever the CFO's name is are sweating bullets because court is in session.)

You have to hand it to Enron and WorldCom. By covering all their bets, records show that these two companies gave Republicans and Democrats money for their election campaigns. These politicians remind you of all those jungle movies where the gorillas stand up and roar, all the while beating their chests. Isn't it time these useless wind bags follow up on their promises and put some pressure on the companies executives and retrieve a majority of the billions of dollars that are sitting in these guys and gals bank accounts drawing interest? If all of this money was put back into an account that was marked for the employees and shareholders, this would help eliminate some of the pain and suffering that these people experience. But, what the heck; the politicians have gotten their money, so it is time to find another cause to boost their opinion polls.

World Policemen

Remember when the Democrats were in control of Congress and the White House and they were sending our young servicemen/women all over the world to stop all of the injustice that was taking place (Bosnia, Somalia, and every other third world sewer)? And who was screaming the loudest to bring these people home - REPUBLICANS, that's who! President Bush is in Africa this week (July 6 –12, 2003) visiting different countries on a fact finding trip and, one of the facts he is looking into is the idea of sending troops into Liberia. The reason the US would send troops into the country is because it is in the middle of a CIVIL WAR. For all of us dumb CCPs the definition of civil war is "War between factions or regions of a single nation."[2] What part of that definition don't our politicians understand? Do any of these fine upstanding educated men and women of Congress and the White House remember their history lessons? How did we get into the Vietnam War? It was when Presidents Eisenhower and Kennedy sent "Military Advisors" over to help in their "Civil War". Why is it, whenever there is a war, the U.S. is the first one invited to join in? Isn't this the responsibility of the useless

---

[2]   Riverside Webster's II New College Dictionary, rev., ed. (1995) "Civil War."

U.N.? We pay all of these billions of dollars yearly to this organization and yet we have to go all over the world to handle their jobs. This is like going to a brothel, walking in the front door, paying your money to the madam, and she tells you to go through that door. You open the door and walk in. The door shuts behind you and it locks then you discover you are in the back yard. Well, you wanted to get screwed and you just did. What I am suggesting is, if the U.S. is going to send military personnel to these countries, then we need to send the U.N. an invoice for all of our work.

Sorry for all of the ranting and raving. If you have not noticed by now, I am not a fan of the U.N. Getting back to the Republicans, they are presently planning to send "Military Advisors" to Liberia. What is that old saying, "If we do not learn from history, we are bound to repeat it."

3.   SPORTS

"To grow old is mandatory, but to grow up is optional" ... A T-Shirt seen in Maui.

CCP Hall of Fame Sports Fan

My father-in-law was the poster boy for the CCP sports fan, a real Jeckyl and Hyde personality type. S. L. "Pep" Whiteside was one of the most respected men in his community; however, this same community did not know that he had been seduced by the dark side and was the ultimate sports fanatic. Within the confines of his home on any given Sunday, there would be a ball game on the television with instructions to the family and the rest of the outside world that he was not to be disturbed. I did not know him at this time, but my wife told me a story that will show you how much of a sports fan he was. It was in September and every CCP knows that, during this time of year, baseball season overlaps with football season. This was not some special occasion. Basically this was a reoccurring event. There would be a crucial game taking place in both the AFC and NFC, so Pep would place the smaller TV on top of the console in the living room. Thus, he would not miss anything important in either game (okay, nothing unusual about this so far, right CCPs?), but he would also have a radio sitting next to his recliner (a.k.a. his command module) listening to the baseball playoffs, while at the same time reading a story in the sports page regarding the heavyweight fight that took place Saturday night. This man had taught his kids correctly; they were not allowed to block his view of the TV at anytime. This included walking in front of the set to go to the bathroom. To relieve the pain in their bladders, the two girls must choose one of two options: 1.) Go out the back door around the house and come in the front door. 2.) Or, low-crawl under the line of sight of the TV (you all have seen movies where soldiers are flat on their stomachs with their rifle cradled in their arms and bullets flying over their heads). And the girls taught their friends how to low-crawl when they visited the house, thus insuring they would see their next birthday.

Pep was such a serious sports fan that when the Seahawks came to Seattle, he bought season tickets and would not miss a home game. I have heard stories from several people regarding the local priest and Pep when the Seahawks were playing away games. It seems that if Father Quinn was getting long-winded and it was getting close to kickoff time, Pep would start looking at his watch on a very regular basis and, being as good-natured as the priest was, he would tell the congregation that he was getting his signal from Pep to cut it short, so the rest of the mass would be performed in a "Reader's Digest" version. As I said earlier, Pep was well respected by everyone that knew him, and the people that did not know him personally also respected him as the Municipal Court Judge of the City of Elma, Washington. Pep was truly loved by everyone and if everyone in the world was like him, this would be a better world to live in. If sports was the only vice we had to worry about, we would mandate every community to have a chapter of Sports Anonymous.

This chapter is going to look at several different sports; and another that is called a sport. It will also look at their players (along with paychecks), the player's attitudes, team owners and the fans. Just in case you skipped the first two paragraphs in this chapter, the word fan was shortened from the root word fanatic. It seems the most important thing that a majority of the players have forgotten is *IT IS A GAME.* As the old saying goes, "The only difference between men and boys is the price of their toys." Living in the Northwest (Washington), I am lucky enough to have several teams (Seahawks, Mariners, Sonics) to watch to enjoy the highs and lows that every sports fan experiences during the different seasons. So when I start discussing these teams' moronic ways of achieving their championship games, it is not that I am a fanatic for the team, but that I get the majority of my information from the local papers and sports on the local news.

Boys Of Summer

I do not have a problem with the idea of free agency for players; lets' face it, every CCP in the country works for a paycheck and if your employer's competitor offered you twice, triple, or quadruple your present salary, you would jump on that offer in a heart beat. Of course there would have to be several clauses in the contract regarding location (war zones definitely qualify as double time), the closest mall location (for the teenagers in the family), and of course, your agent (spouse) would have the final say in the matter. With all of that said, let's look at the exodus of players that have left the Mariners in the last few years and their reasons for leaving.

Randy Johnson is a six-foot ten-inch left-handed pitching machine. Instead of a left arm, God gave him a rocket launcher, and if you think I am exaggerating, take a look at the video where he was pitching in a game and a bird flew between him and the batter. The ball struck the bird in mid-air, knocking the majority of its feathers off and it was dead by the time it hit the ground. I am a good size man myself (6' 8"), but I, personally, would rather sandpaper a wild cat's ass in a phone booth than face one of Mr. Johnson's (in case he reads the book) fast balls high and inside. I might survive the cat, but I am too old and slow to get out of the way of that BB coming at me. You know, I never have faced his fastball and probably never will, but it has to be disheartening to the batters, especially rookies, to hear the sound of the ball pass you in the batters box and hit the catcher's glove. This is an everyday occurrence in baseball; the only problem is that with Mr. Johnson's pitches, the sound is not running simultaneous with the ball. In other words, the catcher is throwing the ball back to Randy (I hope it is OK that I used your first name, Mr. Johnson) when the batter hears the thump of the ball hitting the glove.

Randy Johnson asked the Mariners' front office for more money, the same thing every CCP has done on his or her job, and the front office refused. Randy had been a past winner of the Cy Young award and had winning seasons practically since the beginning of time. The Mariners traded Randy to the Astros where he played for the remainder of the season and at the end of that year, he signed with the expansion team, the Diamondbacks. He now plays in the Big Apple for the dark side, otherwise known as the Yankees. The thing most of us Mariners fans admired about Randy during this whole transition period was his honesty. He wanted more money and felt he should have been paid what other pitchers around the league with his statistics were making. He did not make up some lame excuse (as you will see was the case with some other great excuses in the following paragraphs). It boiled down to "SHOW ME THE MONEY." Since that time, Randy has earned one of those big fancy gold rings that Major League Baseball gives to the winner of the World Series. To date, the only way a Mariner player gets a World Series ring is to be an ex-Mariner and play on another team. The fans were sorry and upset to see Randy leave Seattle, but it was a business deal. When Randy came back to Seattle to pitch in the All-Star game, the fans of Seattle gave him a standing ovation. Randy did not even acknowledge the ovation, and that was wrong. The fans did not screw him over and he seemed to forget the fans were there for the bad years as well as the good ones and they paid a good portion of his salary. If he is pissed at anyone it should be the management, not the fans, so if he ever does come back to Seattle, he needs to take the chip off his shoulder and throw that ball just as hard as he wants to; and guess what? We will still root for him, even if he is throwing a no hitter against us.

Ken Griffey Jr's reason for leaving the Mariners was "to be closer to his family." Mind you, he had a million dollar home in the Seattle area. Being originally from Florida, I understand why his main household is in Orlando. Upon leaving the Mariners, Jr. signed with the Cincinnati Reds. Now it has been documented in the previous chapters that I am not the smartest man alive and that math is not my strongest suit. Please feel free to educate me again with another equation. Orlando is located approximately in the center of the state (east to west) of Florida and is in the southern half. The Tampa Bay Devil Rays are located approximately 90 miles west of Orlando. The Miami Marlins are located 250 miles south of his home. Cincinnati is 900 miles north of his humble abode. I know it is "Fuzzy Math" again and we are missing a few parts of the equations, let's see if I can fill in the blanks. The year of Jr's exodus from Seattle, the Devil Rays and Marlins finished in the cellar of their divisions and the Reds went to the playoffs coming close to going to the World Series. Since Jr. left town, the Mariners have been in the playoffs and the Reds get to watch the playoffs on television. Don't feel sad for Jr. though.

Look at the bright side; he gets to start his golf season earlier than the Mariners' players. See, there is a silver lining in every cloud. The fans of Seattle still feel bitter about the manner in which Jr. left. There was no reason to say he needed to be closer to the family. Unlike Randy Johnson, Jr. has not come back to Seattle even when he had the chance. Feeling guilty? Who knows and further more, who cares?

Alex Rodriguez's (a.k.a. AROD) excuse was the most outrageous statement that has ever been uttered in Seattle. "I want to play for a team that will be in the contention of winning a world series and it is not about money" were the words that AROD said to the local news organizations. AROD's agent was trying to get the Mariners management to agree to bring in the left field fence, thus insuring AROD would have a chance of making baseball history for shortstops hitting the most homeruns for a player at that position. Please do not think I am saying that AROD is trying to cheat or anything like that, because he is one of the greatest ball players to walk on a diamond in my lifetime and undoubtedly will be enshrined in the Baseball Hall of Fame when he retires. The Mariners bent over backwards trying to please AROD and his agent but nothing worked out, so AROD and his agent made a tour of the majority of the baseball parks in the country. When the circus (AROD's entourage) finally set up the big top, it was in the ballpark of the Texas Rangers. Don't those two words, Texas Rangers, send shivers up and down the spine of all the CCP true die-hard baseball fans? I mean, that name belongs right up there in the hallowed halls of baseball history as being a force to be reckoned with, right alongside of the Yankees, Dodgers, Giants, and the Braves. YEAH RIGHT! The Rangers finished so far down in their division that the team saves money on sun tan lotion because sunlight could not go down that deep. And do not forget, it is not about the money; it is about being in contention for the "Holy Grail" of baseball, the World Series ring. As stated previously, a good majority of our CCPs are a little slow, but we are not stupid, and there are 250,000,000 reasons that prove it. $250,000,000 for ten years to play a ball game. There are small countries that will not have that type of income for the same period. You know this is a ridiculous amount of money when my smart-ass way of thinking cannot come up with something to ridicule him. I guess the only thing I can say is **_WOW_**. I have another question I need answering, so please feel free to educate me again (I wonder if I can get college credit for all of this information that is being sent to me?). AROD's contract states that he has to be the highest paid player in baseball. What happens if another player signs a contract more than his and has that same clause in it, where will the numbers end? Where will the money come from? What countries will not receive the foreign aid that was coming to them? Since writing this statement about AROD, he was traded to the "Dark Side" Yankees and the Rangers still have to pay a portion of his salary.

When AROD was in Seattle (after Jr. left), he was the heartthrob of all the young, middle age, and old women, and he was the fair hair child of the team. Basically whatever AROD wanted, AROD got. In other words, the Superstar's, ego was humongous. So the first time he comes to the plate (in SafeCo field) after signing with the Rangers, 50,000 fans start booing and throwing monopoly money (in some case, real money) onto the field. The TV camera zoomed in for a close up and he had this hurt look on his face. What did he expect? Seattle fans had a long meaningful relationship with AROD and he treated us like a one-night stand. And to add insult to injury he flies into town for the ball game and expects the fans to still love him. Grow up AROD, this was not a booty call since we'd already experienced the screwing, this is business. Like the old song said, "Take the money and run." There must be a God because the Mariners fans got to see a small form of justice applied to AROD. The year the Mariners tied the all time record for games won in a single season (116), it all boiled down to one pitch. If the Mariners lost this game they would be one game off the record with the 1906 Chicago Cubs. Picture this: Top of the 9th, two outs, and two strikes on the batter who could end up being the winning run. The pitcher throws the ball, the hitter connects with the ball and it is tipped fouls and the catcher catches the ball. That was nothing spectacular, it happens every day in baseball. It just so happen to be that "Quarters" (as in quarter of a billion dollars) aka AROD was the batter. So AROD now goes into baseball trivia history for being the richest man in baseball and for being the last out in that record game.

In 2002, Major League Baseball came close to having another strike, and everyone agreed that another strike would hurt baseball in such a manner that it may not be able to recover. The last strike left a very bitter taste in the mouths of the fans and the fans were slow coming back to the ballparks. One of the statements made by players showed how they see the world and how us lowly peons pay for it. Edgar Martinez, Super Star DH of the Mariners and really a great man in the Seattle community, stated that one of the sticking points was the minimum salary for a major league player should be $1,000,000, per year. This wage was needed since not every player had a long career and what would happen to him after baseball. ***GET A REAL JOB!*** That is what they should do, game's over, turn out the lights, go back to school and finish the degree you started, and go to work. But then again, what do I know? I am just the master of the remote control in my house.

Grid Iron

Bear with me if my partiality starts showing in these next few paragraphs because football is my favorite sport to watch. It doesn't matter if it is the pros or college just as long as I get to see a wide receiver separated from the ball along with his helmet and jock (and not necessarily that order) as he drags over the middle. This is obviously an ex-linebacker talking. This sport has replaced baseball as America's favorite past time in a big way and look at its history. The first Super Bowl was not a sellout and last years Super Bowl tickets were so expensive that the true reason for the collapse of Enron was that the executives were selling futures and their first born for tickets. The days of old are long gone with the new super stadiums, billionaire owners, mega star players and the insightful agents.

Speaking of agents, this has to be one of the most asinine contracts that have ever been signed in football history. The Seahawks drafted quarterback Rick Mirer from Notre Dame (we could have gotten Drew Bledsoe) as their first round draft pick. After all the haggling and negotiating, a contract was hammered out and signed by both parties, but there was one unusual clause in this legal document. Bear with me; I have not seen it personally, I am relying on news agencies (enough said) but it stated that "If the end of the world came about before the end of the contract, the Seahawks would still be held responsible to pay Rick his money." My question, to Rick and/or his agent, where the hell were you planning on cashing the check if the world as we know it does not exist? Two good things came out of the contract. 1) We did not find out where Rick was going to cash the check because the world did not end. 2) Rick is no longer on the Seahawks payroll.

Take a closer look at the players on a football team. They are all CCP members because of all the hours of sitting on the couch viewing tapes of upcoming games. There have been all kinds of social and psychological studies done on football and the players. And they still have not gotten the simple answer; it is a game where men are going to line up against each other and then beat the hell out of each other. So the following is the CCPs Sigmund Freud's "Reader's Digest" version of football.

Quarterbacks (QB) are the CEO of the playing field corporation and are paid accordingly. They are being paid so much that the NFL has created new rules to prevent them from getting injured. Back in the late 70's when the NFL issued a new rule protecting the QBs, Jack Lambert, linebacker (big, mean) for the Steelers, suggested putting dresses on them. No one made fun of Jack's suggestion, not even his team's QB Terry Bradshaw. Terry was like a Timex watch - he "took a licking and kept on ticking." He was called slow and dumb when he first came into the league. But now they have to give him his dues, Pro Bowler, Hall of Fame member, and the owner of four Super Bowl rings. One thing the world needs to learn about us southern CCPs is just because we talk slow doesn't mean that we are a sandwich shy of a full picnic, isn't that right Mr. Bradshaw? If the NFL wants to protect the QBs, here are a few suggestions for the next rules committee meeting)

In soccer, the goalie wears a different color jersey from the rest of his/her teammates. Same thing could apply here by having the QB wear a different color jersey and make it a color such as Pink, Magenta, Violet, etc. so the defender could not say he had mistakenly hit the wrong person.

The NFL could issue all QBs flags like you find in intramural games; thus insuring no reason the QB would get hit; just pull the flags. Just make sure the flags are a color so the defenders could see them like the ones mentioned above.

Make them wear those blow-up Sumo wrestler suits you find in some bars, but if you employ this rule, defensive lineman (Warren Sapp especially) would not be allowed to dribble the QB back to his end zone for a safety. After the second bounce the QB is down.

These are just a few suggestions, but as stated earlier I used to play linebacker and therefore I agree with Jack Lambert whole heartedly. QBs, if you strap on the helmet and have the ball in your hands, plan on having the following equations done to your body repeatedly during the course of the game: your head in the turf = pain, your ass in the turf = pain, and any other parts of your body in the turf = pain. The common denominator to all of these equations is ***Force*** applied on a regular basis. This is football. Quit making special rules for certain players.

Running backs (RB) would have to be considered the President of the corporation, and thus it is his job to *run* the business and protect the CEO. I am sure there is not a running back in the NFL that can see the comparison I just mentioned while he is trying to pick off Derrick Brookes (outside linebacker of the Bucs) who is bearing down on his QB at the speed of sound. I'm sure when he deflected Brookes to the outside of the pocket and the QB completed the pass for a touchdown, the running back went back to the huddle and began a discussion regarding options and future stocks in the company. RBs are the flashy selfish player. Bottom line; they want the ball every play, that is unless the defensive line is beating the hell out of them, then they want the QB to pass and, if the defensive line is that good, usually the QB is taking a beating. And since the QB is the CEO he delegates the beating to take place on the RB. That's why he is the QB and gets paid the big bucks. The goal of every RB is to rush for a 1,000 yards a season and the ultimate goal is to rush over 2,000 yards in a single season.

The NFL's all time leading rusher is Emmett Smith of the Dallas Cowboys (that was until March 2003; the Cowboys released him) and he is from my hometown of Pensacola, Florida. I was lucky enough to get to watch him play when he was in high school (Escambia High School Gators), then I was upset with him when he went to the University of Florida, being I am a Florida State fan. After high school and college, this young man was always having to prove the critics wrong and it was always the same criticisms. He isn't big enough; he isn't fast enough, blah, blah, blah. Well there is an old saying down south and it says, "It ain't how big the dog is in the fight, it is how much fight is in the dog." Smith was not the fastest RB in the NFL but how many highlight films have you seen him running by Corner Backs (CB) or Safeties (S) looking like a Greyhound in a race with Beagles. And it was very rare if a linebacker ever got a good clean solid hit on him. This was due to his ability to make people miss him. The motivation for this is due to the fact these LBs are big and mean (I mean really mean) and the pain that would follow could surely ruin the following week. Smith could stop on a dime, give you nine cents change, and be going in the opposite direction before you knew what hit you. And number 22 was not just a flashy runner. He is a true ball player; ask Troy Aikman how many times Smith saved his bacon from blitzing LBs or Ss. Emmett was one of the major reasons Troy did not enter broadcasting earlier than he did.

Offensive Linemen (OL) are the most underrated people on the team. These guys would be your blue-collar workers. As John Madden has said, "They show up with their lunch pails and go to work." In this day and time, these guys are so big the lunch pail has been replaced with an "Igloo" cooler (you know the type, it has wheels). The majority of the time a lineman only gets his number called because he is guilty of a penalty, such has holding, clipping, kicking, biting, spitting, and other socially unacceptable acts (I did not like linemen in my playing days), so to fit the linemen in a category everyone can understand, they are the Rodney Dangerfield of the NFL. Linemen are family and they will do everything in their power to protect the QB, (including the offenses mentioned in the prior sentence), and shove people out of the way to make a hole for the RB to get through. And it is about time these guys start making some of the big contracts. If it was not for this group of men (notice I didn't use the word "gentle", as in "gentlemen"), the game of football would be like the game all boys played when they were young, Kill the Guy with the Ball.

Wide Receivers (WR) have to be the salesmen of the organization. You know the type. They want to be the center of attention. They are running down the field with their hand in the air screaming that they are open, but in reality they have three defenders hanging on them like a cheap suit. But you can rest assured when he gets back to the huddle he will inform the QB he was open and had them beat by a mile. If you look back in history, you will find that it was WRs that started the "Disco Era" in the end zone after a touchdown. Kind of reminds you of those flashy used car ads with the balloons, animals and some really bad actor yelling, "Come on down and see how great I am!!" Most of the WRs in the NFL barely can *spell* "block", much less apply one, but then you find a player that defies the laws of nature, and that player's name is Jerry Rice. At 40 years old, he should be on the golf course enjoying the fruits of his labor, not having his wife playing connect the bruises on Monday morning. The man has such a rigid off-season workout it would put mere mortals in traction, and this is the main reason he is still playing today. (He finally retired in 2005.) There must be some secret trick he's using to keep playing, but he is not telling. If you watch a Raiders game you will see all of the water and Gatorade coolers on the table, and if you notice closely, there is one at the end of that table that only Jerry drinks from. I do not know this for a fact, but I have been told it is filled with Geritol.

Kickers are just plain strange and are a necessary evil. As Popeye used to say, "You can't live with them and you can't live without them." The offense is run as a well-oiled machine, and everything is built around timing, And the kicking game is part of the offense. Enough said.

The defense, on the other hand, carries the responsibility to disrupt the offense's timing. If you know a defensive player, beware, because this man's job is a legalized form of chaos and mayhem, along with thievery. Most of the defensive players are the type of people that would attend church, wearing band-aids backwards so that when the offering plate is passed around, it would *look* as if they were placing money in the plate. The main purpose for the defense is to prevent the offense from getting a first down; no first downs, and zero scores. In the process of preventing the offense from reaching a first down, the defense will do everything in its power (legal or not) to get the ball back. Separating the ball from the carrier is the number one priority of the defense. If in the process of separation (ball/ carrier) the helmet, shoes, mouthpiece, teeth, nose, arms or legs come with the ball, so be it.

Defensive Linemen (DL) are big, mean, fast, and those are their good characteristics. Once these guys put on their helmets and button up their chin straps, you will hear sound coming out of the beings that are not human (and the mindset to go all with the sounds). Anyone that does not believe in alien abduction or demon possession has never stood shoulder pad to shoulder pad to one of these men (and I am using that word loosely) prior to them entering the game. The primary job of a DL is to get to the person with the ball, be it QB or RB, and remove said ball from the persons of said ball carrier in any manner the DL sees fit. Except the DL cannot grab that great handle that is attached to the helmet called a facemask (voice of experience speaking: grab that handle and you can stop the ball carrier in a heartbeat). The secondary job is to put pressure on the QB if it is a pass play and their other roles of responsibility are to stop the run and keep the OL off the linebackers. Warren Sapp should be considered the Darth Vader of the NFL. He is the prototype of the first sentence describing DLs. This man talks so much trash that whatever town he plays in, the garbage workers demand double time to clean up after him, and the bad thing about it is that he backs up everything he says he is going to do. Any OL that lines up against Warren on Sunday knows the following things are true: 1) Sunday is going to be a long day, 2) Monday will be a painful experience, 3) There will be a lot of laughter and whistles while watching the game film and seeing how bad Warren made him look. And if that OL is lucky, his team is not in the same division with the Bucs and will not have to face Warren again for a long time.

Linebackers (LB) are basically paid assassins; picking and choosing where they are going to deliver a world of hurt on a ball carrier. The LB mentality is this: If the ball carrier is going to cross the line of scrimmage, he had better give his heart to the Lord because his ass is mine. Remember that line in the Bible that says, "Revenge is mine sayth the Lord"? Well, sometimes he is a little busy, so LBs help him out, and they definitely love the "vengeance" part. The recruiting poster for LBs would have Dick Butkus and Mike Singletary on it. When these two men strapped on their helmets, no one carrying a football was safe… man, woman, or child. There was a reason they called the Bears defense the "Monsters of the Midway", and these two Hall of Fame players were the anchors of those teams. I heard a coach make the following statement "To be a linebacker you have to be mean or crazy and in most cases it helps to be both."

Defensive Backs (DB) includes Corner Backs (CB) and Safeties (Free & Strong). If these guys were not on the field, they could be excellent pickpockets or burglars. If the QB throws a pass, the DBs will do everything under the sun to steal that ball (some of it is legal and some not so legal, but what the heck; keep doing it until you get caught). Just because the WR catches the ball does not mean the DBs are going to allow him to keep it. The DBs are going to hit that WR like a pack of sharks in a feeding frenzy pushing, shoving, hitting, and trying to strip the ball from the WR and if the ball comes loose before the WR hits the ground the DBs win. One of the best CBs to play that position was "Prime Time" Deion Sanders. If a QB saw his receiver had three steps on Prime Time and was stupid enough to throw the ball to that receiver, ring the bell because school is in session. Sanders would put on a burst of speed, intercept the ball and be running for a touchdown before the QB could get the first cuss word out of his mouth. I have been told that Prime Time is so fast that he can stand at the door to his bedroom, turn out the light and be in the bed before the room is dark. Now that's fast!

Warren Sapp recently said, "It is a kids game and we are getting a kings ransom to play it." Mr. Sapp is correct. It is a game. It is not a life and death struggle and maybe some of the players and fans should remember that.

The Links

This is the game of choice for a good majority of us old, slow and overweight CCPs. We have finally learned that we do not heal as fast as we used to when we were younger. After a game of basketball, football, or baseball we could be in pain for months but after a round of golf, the hangover the next morning is usually gone by noon. Things have definitely changed in the world of golf in the last fifty years. An example of that is the public executions by the fashion police at Pebble Beach in the late 70's made the golfers dress as if someone with an IQ larger than their handicap helped them get dressed. There is always an exception to the crowd and the present exception is Sweden's Jasper Parnevik, he still wears bright skin-tight clothes. His pants are so tight they could be compared to a cheap hotel, no ballroom. Get your mind out of the gutter. By no ballroom, I am talking about what the majority of golfers do, and that is having an extra ball in his back pocket. He could not get a ball in his pocket unless his caddy slipped a shoe spoon in the pocket and then placed his knee in the small of Parnevik's back and then pried the material apart with all of his strength. I do not know why he wears these clothes while wearing the bill of his cap bent up toward the sky. There may be a couple of reasons he dresses this way. Maybe it's because he is European and all American CCPs know they dress funny over there. Maybe it's because his father is the most famous comedian in Sweden and he is practicing his routine on us before going back to Sweden. But rest assured the fashion police have outstanding warrants on him and the next one they are targeting is Charles Howell III (the skinny kid).

The biggest change in golf can be summed up in the following joke that was sent to me. Years ago when 100 white men chased 1 black man, it was called the Klu Klux Klan; today it is called the PGA tour. Tiger Woods has introduced golf to a new group of players that normally would not have even thought about picking up a golf club. Tiger is definitely the newest ambassador of golf. In the 60's it was Arnold Palmer with "Arnie's Army" and in the 70's it was Jack Nicklaus and his following of fans. In the 80's and the first half of the 90's there was not one clear champion of the PGA tour. It seemed the golf world had reached parity. Every week there was a different winner, and golf on TV was something you watched if there was not a good infomercial on. Then a young man that had been molded for greatness in golf came onto the scene, after telling the NCAA to basically shove it because Arnold Palmer had paid for his dinner one night and they expected Tiger to pay him back. The rules of the NCAA are out of touch with reality, and that could be a book in and of itself. Tiger came onto the PGA tour like his name states... with a roar.

Everyone and anyone that followed golf knew this young man was going to give golf a shot in the arm and boost its ratings, but no one knew the shot was going to be administered with an ICBM. Of course Tiger made rookie mistakes his first year on the tour, but he won a tournament, and his second year he was still in a learning curve. Ring the bell, boys, because school is in session. Tiger learned the lessons well because the next three years it looked like he was at recess. He was just playing with the remainder of the players in any given tournament. It seemed that all of the other players were jockeying for second place in any tournament that Tiger participated in. Tiger has definitely raised the bar in golf and instead of rolling over and being happy with second place, the other players have starting working hard to achieve the goals that Tiger has set. It seemed for a while that the other players were believing everything they read in the papers about Tiger, and I am here to set the record straight. A good amount of you golfers may have seen the cover of Golf Digest with Tiger hitting a ball off of a pond as if to show he could walk on water. Well, he cannot walk on water, but he is dry from his knees up.

I guess my only complaint about professional golfers is their Prima Donna attitude they have toward silence while hitting the ball. I mean it is not like that little white ball is going to jump off the tee and come at them with the speed of a Randy Johnson fastball. Recently, a photographer took a picture while Tiger was hitting a ball, when all of a sudden, all hell broke loose. Tiger's caddy jumped over the rope grabbed the man's camera and threw it in a lake. Thank God this is a gentleman's game. I would hate to see what would have happened if all this action took place at a hockey game. First of all, if I had been that photographer, I would have never taken the picture, but if by accident it happened, when Tiger's caddy had jumped the rope he would have had the time of his life. Supposedly he is an adrenalin junkie, but trust me, you grab me and I am going to give you your daily fix of adrenalin. How many baseball players demand the stands be quiet before the pitcher releases the ball. You know Barry Bonds has wanted to go up in the stands, especially when playing the Mets in New York, with his bat and make some fans be quiet. If he can hit a fastball, curve, slider, and a change up with 50,000 people screaming and cussing, what is the problem with the golfers hitting a stationary ball. Before becoming a pro golfer, every PGA player played with friends and not so friendly competitors in school or for a friendly bet and was hassled during a round. If other ball players can handle noise, maybe the golfers need to get the telephone numbers of their co-professionals' sports psychiatrist.

Golf coverage has gotten to an all-time high and there are enough golf publications printed each month that causes small forests to be clear cut to provide the paper. Then you have the golf channel that will supply your daily fix of golf information. Whether it is golf history, facts, layout of courses, equipment ads, or how to improve your game, it is right there, twenty four hours a day, seven days a week. As previously mentioned, I am an avid golfer, playing as many times a year as I can without having to see a divorce attorney, and I like keeping up on what is happening in the golf world, but some of the reporters that are covering the pro tour need to get a reality check.

In the next chapter you will see what I think about the news industry as a whole. In case you skip that chapter, I will some it up for you, "I think the entire group is lower than a whale crap at the bottom of the ocean". It seems the reporting of sports is moving in the same direction that news coverage has been in for the last twenty years. It is going to the "Dark Side" or extreme negative views. And here are two prime examples.

Recent headlines in most publications or TV coverage: "TIGER WOODS IN A SLUMP". What is wrong with this picture? The young man has just recently turned thirty and the golf gurus are screaming his demise and are ready to bury him. Just because he has not won every outing he has played in this year does not mean rigormortis has set in. There are some outside forces that they seem to forget about. Tiger had knee surgery in the winter and had to endure a good amount of physical therapy to get his lower body back in shape before the season began. What you non-golfers do not understand is that the lower portion of your body plays an important part of your game with all of the twisting and bending that is required to hit the ball. And let's not forget, these guys have to walk the course, since the PGA thinks golf carts is the major reason the country's morals has reached an all time low. On the average, a golf course on the men's tournament is over 7,000 yards, which equals out to be 3.97 miles (for the sake of argument, I will round it off to 4 miles), and this is the yardage they play. It does not count the territory they have to cover walking from one green to the next tee and in some cases this can be a long stroll. Now a full tournament is played, which adds up to four days and the player has just walked 16 + miles, in heat, cold, rain and every type of weather condition known to man. The young man has just come off knee surgery and he wins the first tournament he plays in. So he does not win the next twelve in a row, give him a break.

Now let's add another factor into this equation. Tiger is playing with new equipment. Nike is Tiger's largest endorsement and the company is now producing golf equipment, balls, gloves, shoes and now clubs. No one ever buys or receives, in this case, new clubs and begins playing at the same level you were at with your old clubs. There is a little thing called a learning curve and it does not happen over night. Now if you believe these doomsday proclaimers that "TIGER

IS IN A SLUMP", I hope I can be so lucky because so far this year he has won over $3,000,000. He has more tax write offs than the majority of the sports writer's salaries and he has to put up with their constant whining. Just one time I would like to see Tiger pull out a check for second, third, tenth or whatever place and compare it to one of the writers' paycheck and then see who was in a slump.

I was watching the reporters grill Tiger after a round one day and the majority of them keep bringing up the S (Slump) word and you could just see the frustration in his face. And you know he would love to tell them where they could go with that line of thought, but he did not. Tiger, just in case you do read this book here is a suggestion for you. The next time you are on the practice range and you see one of the annoying reporters, wait for him to bend over to pick up something, then take a five iron and fire a line drive up his back side (not back nine) and the next time he asks you about your slump you can tell him, "If you are going to ask the same dumb questions that you are pulling out of your ass, while you are in there, would you mind retrieving my ball?" (It is just a thought, and up to you.) One important factor that these reporters seem to have over looked is the other players on the tour. It seems they may have gotten tired of fighting for second place and done some things in the off season to change things. This year Tiger is not leading the long drive average or any of the other statistics that are kept. Players are taking this game serious now by changing their diets, working out, equipment modifications and mentally getting themselves ready to play Tiger, and not just giving him the tournament. So, to answer the questions for Tiger, no, he is not in a slump; he is in a tournament where any given player can win. Just ask Ben Curtis. Who is he, you ask? Ben just won the British Open on Sunday, July 20, 2003 and prior to the tournament, he was rated 396 in the world rankings for professional golfers. Note: Tiger resumed his winning streak in 2004 with a new green jacket (The Masters) and is not looking back.

The other asinine thing that a majority of the sports writers dwell on is "He has never won a MAJOR". For all of you non-golfers, there are four tournaments that are considered a major: the Masters, the US Open, the British Open and the PGA Tournament. It seems that these reporters do not think these other tournaments amount to very much. Maybe I was wrong about these guys' and girls' paychecks, because the winner of any given tournament wins damn near a million dollars and, in some tournaments, over a million. I do not know about you guys, but where I come from, earning a million dollars for four days of work is very impressive. And it seems these reporters always focus on one player until he wins a major or falls from their graces. This pressure was put on Davis Love, David Duvall, Colin Montgomery and Phil Mickelson. To bring you up to date, Davis and David have each won a major, Colin is a foreigner, so no one cares, and that leaves Phil. The pressure that is being placed on this young man by a bunch of athletic supporters is ridiculous. This is the same group of people that could not play a sport in school, so they joined the high school paper and wrote about them. And today, nothing has changed but their waistlines and hair lines, as in bigger in one area and littler in the other.

Phil has won over twenty tournaments and is a multimillionaire and has his life in perspective. He has a beautiful wife, two little girls and a new baby boy - now what is wrong with this picture? He has the American dream and he has a group that is not happy with his success. What is wrong with this picture? The man's name will go down in golf's history books as one of the times best golfers for his period, whether or not he wins a major, and furthermore, he does not give a damn what the writers think. And I think that is what disturbs the writers the most. Phil is not intimidated by the press; furthermore he is not intimidated by the PGA. A couple of years ago, Phil was in contention for the US Open, and during the entire time he was playing, he had a pager with him. The reason for the pager was due to the fact his wife was about to give birth to one of their children, and he let it be known that if the pager went off, he was out of there (Phil did not win and the pager did not go off). This did not sit well with the press or the PGA, but Phil did not care about the tournament, the press, the PGA or none of those other non-important things in his life. His family was the most important thing that matters, not a GAME! People, it is only a game! It is not a life and death matter; we will not go to war if he does not play, the economy will not bottom out (trust me, this recession is not Phil's fault), or any of the other plaques that the press can come up with. Mr. Mickelson, if the rest of the country had their perspectives in order the way you do, there would be fewer problems in this country. So for all of you reporters that keep screaming at Phil to win a major, get off your dead ass, earn your PGA tour card, and take your chances in the pressure cooker and win a major. After you win the major, then you have a right to jump on his ass; till then, shut the hell up. Since writing this section Phil has won the Masters and the PGA Tournament.

The Masters

Confucius once said, "It is better to remain silent and thought of as a fool than to open one's mouth and remove all doubt." And for the most part, all of our CCPs are seeing this proverb come true on national television regarding the debacle (I mean debate) of the membership of the Augusta National Country Club. Augusta National is a male-only club where the "Holy Grail" of golf is played every April and that tournament's name is "The Masters." In June of 2002, Ms. Martha Burk, the chair of the National Council of Women's Organizations, wrote Mr. William "Hootie" Johnson asking/demanding that Augusta National cease being a male-only club. In the letter, Ms. Burk's knowledge of golf showed that it would fit on the head of a tee. I am not saying this because I am a knuckle dragging Neanderthal anti-feminist. Oh, to the contrary, I will present proof, and this proof will come from the mouth of babes (I just had to throw that in being the knuckle dragging un-PC person I am). No, the babes I am talking about is the one and only Martha Burk. Once all hell broke out between her and Hootie (don't you just love that name?), she stated, "An event of this profile could be held somewhere else." Then another statement was issued saying she would put pressure on the PGA to move the tournament. Now here are the problems with those two statements. The first is, "The Masters" is put on by Augusta National and it is one of the four "Major" tournaments. The second being, the PGA has no rights to the Masters since it is not a PGA sponsored tournament. As my father told me one time, "Before you go shooting your mouth off, make sure your ammunition is not blanks. Think before you speak and know what you are talking about." I guess you could say Martha had a bad case of Hoof & Mouth disease (get off your soap box, I am not knuckle dragging again. I will show you later that Hootie has a good case of Mad Cow disease himself). Next phase of her attack was to pressure the players to boycott the Masters. Martha dear, these guys would rather miss their own mother's funeral than miss a chance at winning the "Green Jacket." Note to Martha: that is the prize the winner gets for winning, along with a whole bunch of money, and one pen will not contain enough ink for all of the endorsement contracts that comes with winning the Masters. The next phase of the attack was to boycott the advertisers that had contracts with Augusta National. Hootie bypassed her on this one. He released all of the advertisers out of their contracts and the

Masters will be shown this year, 2003, without commercials. Augusta National is a for-profit corporation and has the money to hold the tournament without sponsors. There is a down side to this. All of the local charities that received money from the sponsors in the past will suffer due to this debacle/debate. Jesse Jackson stated, "The gender bigotry is as offensive as racial bigotry or religious bigotry."[3] And here is a news flash. Jesse Jackson is going to hold a demonstration during the week of the Masters. Let's face it, Jackson would show up to the opening of an envelope if it got his picture on the evening news. Here is a tidbit of useless information: when Martha Burk was younger her nickname was, you guessed it, "Hootie." What about that old statement "Politics makes strange bedfellows"? If they have the same nickname, would that make it incest?

Being raised in the South, I have known my fair share of guys named Bubba, Cooter, Catfish, Horny, Stinky, but I have never met a Hootie. And what I am about to say is a sure bet: I will never meet the one that runs Augusta National. For all of you CCPs that are not golf aficionados (notice how I slipped that big word for fan in there), let me give you a "Readers Digest" version of the history of Augusta National. The club is run by the "Blue Bloods" of the South. No one applies for membership, you are asked to become a member. When the invoice for the dues is mailed to you, pay it and don't worry what the bill is because it is like that old saying "If you have to ask how much, you can't afford it." In the past it was a segregated club, but recently they have seen the error of their ways and have allowed minorities in the hallowed halls of the clubhouse; and approximately 4% of the members are minorities. They didn't exactly open the floodgates, did they?

---

[3] David Owen, "The Case For The All-Male Golf Clubs" <u>Golf Digest</u> March 2003, 112

The "Holy Trinity" of Augusta National is Bobby Jones (legendary golfer), **Mr.** Cliff Roberts (not the actor, and do not forget the *Mister* portion of his name) and Hootie. Roberts and Hootie have run Augusta National in the same manner as some dictators have run third world countries, only they do not have the power to shoot dissenters (trust me, they looked into the local laws). If you are a member and you break one of the unwritten rules, also known as the flavor of the month, you will be sent to golf purgatory and you will know you have arrived there when your next year club's dues invoice does not arrive at your home. I am a believer of tradition, but to a point. Look what tradition did to the British during the Revolutionary War, standing in straight lines screaming at the American rebels hiding behind trees to come out an fight like true gentlemen. Results, Non-Traditionalist - 1, Traditionalist – 0. Years later the score changed to 2 - 0 after the war of 1812. Mr. Roberts has gone to that big sand trap in the sky, so nowadays Hootie runs the show. Augusta does not come out and demand certain things; they just make a suggestion in such a manner as to let you know who is in charge. Such as CBS, the network that covers the Masters, must call all of the people attending the tournament "patrons" not fans, and God forbid one of their announcers says something discouraging about the course. Gary McCord was on the air one time talking about how fast the greens were when he said the greens were not cut short by Augusta National, instead they "used bikini wax on them." After that, McCord was never allowed to cover the Masters with CBS. Augusta would not tell CBS that he could not be part of their crew, but they wanted to see the list of names of the anchors working the tournament and McCord's name should not be on the list.

Hootie could have responded to Martha's letter in a more PC manner (and you people thought I was PC ignorant; you have just met the Poster Boy for *un-PC*). The last time I looked,

God hasn't died and left Hootie in charge. This is not the 1950's and there are ways to negotiate changes without having a pissing contest in public. Both sides have handled this affair badly, and now there is no room for compromise. I play golf on a regular basis with my wife and my daughter and personally, I would not want either one of them to be a member. I know the odds of me ever playing a round at Augusta are higher than any formula that Einstein ever worked with and the odds of a woman being admitted while Hootie is in power are more than likely the same. I am not for either side in this power struggle because it is not going to affect my world, but I recently read an article in Golf Digest that makes you stop and think. The following is an excerpt from that article.

The Case For All-Male Golf Clubs

"I infuriated a woman I know by showing her the following excerpts from a statement by Hootie Johnson, the chairman of Augusta National Golf Club:

While men's golf clubs are diverse, their members have a common desire to create sustained bonds with other men. . . . Men's golf clubs, through their enduring presence, offer a sense of rootedness, a common body of experience and knowledge, a sense of continuity.... We are forever being told to give more energy, more time, to our marriage, our career, our children, our community. Men's golf clubs tell us to spend more time with our male friends.

"What a stinking bunch of sexist junk," she said. (I'm paraphrasing-believe me.) So I infuriated her again by confessing that Johnson hadn't actually said those things, and that I'd lifted them, with the minor modifications, from the introduction of a popular recent book called *Girls' Night Out; Celebrating Women's Groups Across America,* by Tamara Kreinin and Barbara Camens. (In the parts I quoted, I substituted "men" for "women" and "male " for "female," and "golf clubs" for "groups.") "That's different," my woman friend said. (I'm paraphrasing again.) Well, is it?"[4]

To give you an insight as to how fair and, God forbid, "Politically Correct" the PGA is, in 1945 Babe Zaharias was allowed to compete in the Los Angeles Open. In May of 2003, the Colonial Open that will be held at the Colonial Country Club in Ft. Worth, TX, will allow Annika Sorenstam, LPGA top money winner in 2002, to participate in the tournament. Update: Annika played the Colonial and did not make the cut. Why isn't Ms. Burk starting a protest movement against the LPGA, since this organization has its own exclusionary charter itself? Only women can be members and only women can be LPGA-certified teaching and club professionals. And to top it off, in November of 2002, Ty Votaw endorsed Martha Burk's war against Augusta National. For all of you CCPs that are not up to date with all of the famous names in the golf world, it is education time again. Ty Votaw is the Commissioner of the LPGA and here is something that will blow your skirt up: Ty is a man. What is wrong with this picture? He can control the LPGA but he cannot be a card-carrying member of the LPGA? Come on Ty, what is fair for one group should be fair for the other. What if we promised you that all of the guys that entered your tournaments would wear outfits that were color coordinated and Jasper Parnevik would not be allowed near the golf course? We all know that on Sundays Tiger wears his power-red shirts, so we could dial it down a little, and when he is on the LPGA he will wear pink. Maybe Peter Jacobsen in shorts (earth tone colors of course) with ankle socks with the little fuzzy ball on the top and Phil Mickelson's wife could dress him in matching outfits with his two daughters. Come on Ty, your gals can play in the boys sand box, why is your playground off limits?

---

[4]   David Owen, "The Case For The All-Male Golf Clubs" <u>Golf Digest </u>March 2003, 113.

For all of you CCPs that are taking physics, here is a question you've seen on tests before that is being played out for the public to watch: the unmovable object (Hootie) meets the unstoppable force (Martha). Who knows the answer to this debacle/debate; it may rewrite the physics books. I guess we will all have to wait to see how this soap opera plays out. You know someone will buy the movie rights. Here is the title "Hootie gets Martha's Panties in a Wad" and the sequel could be "Martha De-Pants Hootie." The sad part to this whole debacle/debate is that Hootie is the spitting image of my first cousin "Wewa."

NASCAR
(Non Athletic Sport Centered Around Rednecks)

I am more than likely one of a handful of southerners that doesn't follow stock car racing. About the only things I know about this sport is the drivers are continually turning left and they have their own Union 76 full service gas station (and the service is really fast). These drivers are pushing the cars at such speeds that g-forces are being exerted on the drivers as in the same manner it is with fighter pilots. The biggest difference between drivers and pilots is when there is an "oops," the pilots can pull an ejection handle, but the drivers have to ride it out. And sometimes those "oops" rides by the drivers are spectacular enough to make the evening news. I was watching a show one time that was featuring a race in which a camera and microphone were inside Darrell Waltrip's car. Darrell is just coming out of a turn and has the pedal to the metal in the straight away when all of a sudden his right front wheel leaves the car and starts rolling off toward the viewing stands. When he sees this happening he breaks out singing a Kenny Roger's song, "You picked a fine time to leave me Lucille", and remember, he is traveling at speeds in excess of 150 mph. As the car travels the length of the straight-a-way, he looks at the approaching curve (trust me the curve is approaching really fast), and he begins saying "This is going to hurt, this is going to hurt" and after watching the crash I am sure it did hurt. Now that is one cool human being. If I had been driving that car, they would have had to mute the audio portion of the broadcast because it would have been embarrassing listening to all of the screaming, crying, and cussing. And that would have just been the portion where the wheel left the car; watching that wall at the other end of the straight-a-way coming at me would definitely qualify as a "Pucker Check Time." For all of you educated sophisticated CCPs that do not know what a pucker check is, let me add to your on-going education. Anytime in life that you can see your possible demise, there will be an involuntary muscle reaction. This is where the muscles in your ass squeeze so tight that a person would not be able to drive a needle up your butt with a 16 lbs. sledgehammer. There have been reported cases where pilot's parachutes had an extra hole in them after ejecting. Remember, in an ejection seat the pilots are strapped into their parachute (and after the follow up medical exams, fabric pieces were pried from the pilot's ass). There have been cases reported with drivers of cars whereupon leaving the car there is a hole in the upholstery. Then, there are the other types of reactions, such as when the driver hits the wall or flips a dozen times, the automatic fire extinguishers are discharged; the driver sometimes helps the extinguishers out by discharging him/herself. For a sport that came out of the hills of the Carolinas running moon shine, they have come a long way and become very profitable at the same time.

Have you ever noticed that the traffic in big cities is very light on the weekends? It is not because everyone is not working. It is because all of the rubber-neckers are at home watching the wrecks on TV and they are some kind of spectacular wrecks. Let's face it; everyone will stop what they are doing and watch one of these cars flip 10 or 12 times and think, "wow", that's cool! All right everyone; but it is the driver of the car that is defying the laws of gravity. The thing that amazes me is the majority of the drivers climb out of the wreck as cool as the under side of a pillow. If that was me climbing out of that wreckage, which there are no parts resembling an automobile, I would be shaking so bad I would be able to thread a sewing machine while it was running. Truly all the people of NASCAR are frosty.

Hockey

I am definitely not an expert on this sport, but I have just one question **What the Hell** is the world coming to when the State of Florida has a hockey team? In the off-season, is the ring thawed and used for water polo?

Synchronized Swimming

Who was the genius that stated this was a sport and had the power to get this water ballet in the Olympics as an event? The most any of us CCPs have gotten to know about Synchronized Swimming (SS) is by watching an old Ethel Mermen movie as she dives into the pool singing about how in love she is, and by the way, there are fifteen of her best girl friends swimming with her. Was this some type of therapy that was used back in the 40's? How can you call this a sport? What type of penalties can these swimmers fear? Too much hair gel, nose clip clashes with your bathing suit? Give me a break! Put another team in the water at the same time and see if the home team can do their routine while the "visitors" are trying to untie their hair, pull their nose clips off, or throw one or two players out of the pool. You know what I am saying here. This is one so-called sport you will never see on Fox's Best Damn Sports

Show Period. Well, unless one of the swimmers swims out of her bathing suit, we would never see the picture, because one of the host would be hogging the screen. Can a player be ejected from the game? And if a penalty occurs, do they have to move to the shallow end of the pool? If you want to make it a sport, how about a penalty box (hockey is a good example) but make sure the box is located at the bottom of the pool?

4.   NEWS

"There is no room in this country for hyphenated Americans. The one absolutely certain way of bringing this nation to ruin, of preventing all possibility of it continuing to be a nation at all, would be to permit to become a tangle of squabbling nationalities."… Theodore Roosevelt, 1915

Some of you CCPs may want to skip this chapter since it will not be that funny and can be quite disturbing. When we are lead down a path of doom and gloom by the people that are supposed to be reporting the truth, by putting such a "SPIN" on it, and in such a manner that it could piss off the Pope, trust me my feelings won't be hurt if you skip ahead.

When did the news quit being the news and when did it become a market rating grabbing production? How many times have you seen the news reporters working up facial expressions to convey the idea that they are really concerned with what they are reporting when, in fact, all they are worried about is getting their air time and you are watching their network. How many times have we seen a reporter shove a microphone in someone's face and somewhere in the background is a picture of a burning house? Then you hear the question, "What is going through your mind at this very moment as you watch your house burn to the ground?" Just once I wish the victim's answer would be shown, because you know someone has told them the truth. "I want to shove that microphone down your throat and pull it out your ass, how do you think I feel?" Why is it that the news anchors for the big networks are demanding that their reporters not wear US Flag pins on their coats? They are afraid that might offend someone by showing partiality. Give me a frigging break... they do it every night with their slanted spin of the news. For once, why don't they try to appease the ignorant masses (that is how they see all of the CCPs), that live, work, and pay their outrageous salaries in America. Who in the US are they worried about offending? If you live in American and the sight of a US Flag offends you, I got one simple solution: **GET THE HELL OUT.** Problem solved! The big time news-readers forget one important thing, and that is that the ignorant masses are the ones that pay their salaries. We have to watch some of the stupidest commercials in the world, over and over again; kind of reminds you of the needle stuck in a groove on one of those ancient things called a record) and these advertisers pay big bucks to be on the evening news. This money pays their salaries. What if the CCPP (Political Party) took a page out of Jesse Jackson's handbook and boycotted the advertisers until we saw a flag pin in the lapel. Can't you see it now... Peter, in an American flag shirt, Dan, with a flag tattoo, and Tom with a flag tie. Oh, and of course, a flag in the background with a fan blowing hard enough to create a hurricane so it would be flapping in the breeze.

The Fourth Estate

The term "fourth estate" is frequently attributed to the nineteenth century historian Carlyle, though he himself seems to have attributed it to Edmund Burke:

> *Burke said there were Three Estates in Parliament; but, in the Reporters' Gallery yonder, there sat a Fourth Estate more important than they all. It is not a figure of speech, or a witty saying; it is a literal fact.... Printing, which comes necessarily out of Writing, I say often, is equivalent to Democracy: Invent Writing, Democracy is inevitable. ..... Whoever can speak, speaking now to the whole nation, becomes a power, a branch of government, with inalienable weight in law-making, in all acts of authority. It matters not what rank he has, what revenues or garnitures: the requisite thing is that he have a tongue which others will listen to; this and nothing more is requisite.*
>
> Carlyle (1905) pp. 349-350

Carlyle here was describing the newly found power of the man of letters, and, by extension, the newspaper reporter. In his account, it seems that the press is the new fourth estate added to the three existing estates, as they were conceived of at the time, running the country: priesthood, aristocracy and commons. Other modern commentators seem to interpret the term fourth estate to mean the fourth 'power' which checks and counterbalances the three state 'powers' of executive, legislature and judiciary.[5]

---

[5] Carlyle: Mass Media: fourth estate – Back Mass Media, Pluralist View. www.cultsock.ndirect.co.uk/MUHome/cshtml/media/4estate.html

Now don't you feel so much smarter after that history lesson? I know I do. If I was one of the high and mighty television news anchors, I would have to give equal page space to the spokesperson that would tell you that I am neglecting the fifth, sixth, and who knows how many other estates (contrary to popular belief, Texas does not fall into this category). Then these same newspersons would explain to you in great detail what you just read. You have to remember that not all CCPs are the brightest people on the planet, so the news organizations have taken it upon themselves to educate the masses instead of stating the facts. What happened to the days of Edwin R. Murrow method of telling the news? When Mr. Murrow told the news it was Who, What, When and Where, basically it was Joe Friday's (Dragnet) "Just the facts Ma'am." I guess no one has told these storytellers that all of us CCPs are not interested in their opinions, just the news. In case any one of these news people read this book (whether in the bathroom or a closet so they will not be seen), let me educate you since you obviously have forgotten this statement. Opinions are like assholes. Everyone has one, but it is only important to you. Enough of history lessons and preaching, now its hunting season on the news organizations in the same fashion I went after the politicians (feel free to jump in here with any good stories you may have regarding these enlightened people).

Truth Be Damned

Does the name Richard Jewell ring a bell? How about that old saying "Except for the grace of God go I?" Richard Jewell was the "hero" that found the backpack that contained a bomb on July 27, 1996, at the Centennial Olympic Park in Atlanta, Georgia. The Atlanta police was warned by an anonymous caller that there was a bomb in the park just minutes before the explosion. Jewell found the pack and tried to move people out of the area before it exploded. One person died and multitudes were injured with Richard being declared a "hero" for the time being. Then the almighty FBI (Fumbling Bunch of Idiots), jump into the scene (examples: Ruby Ridge, Waco, 9/11) said that Richard fits a profile, so he became "THE SUSPECT". The blood trail is in the water, so here come the sharks. The press jumped on this story like a new tattoo on Dennis Rodman. There was not one bit of evidence linking him to the bombing, but as the ever-enlightened one from NBC, Tom Brokaw, said, "Look, they probably got enough to arrest him. They probably have got enough to try him." Brokaw has since emphasized that he finished his on-air remarks by saying: "Everyone, please understand absolutely he is only the focus of this investigation – he is not even a suspect yet."[6] Jewell was cleared on October 26, 1996. Therefore, for eighty-eight days, this mans life was a living hell.

Mr. Jewell's attorney (this is truly hard rooting for an attorney) L. Lin Wood Jr. stated in such a manner that everyone would understand, "We're going to sue everyone from A to Z." Not only did he sue NBC, he went through the alphabet and got the rest of the vultures. ABC, CBS, CNN, The Atlanta Journal-Constitution, and even local radio stations that carried the story were subjected to lawsuits. Mr. Jewell did an outstanding job by saving as many people as he did that night, at great risk to himself, but no amount of money will ever remove the asterisk by his name when anyone mentions the Olympic bombing incident. It seems the news organizations forgot that the founding fathers drafted the Constitution in such a manner that a person is innocent until they are proven guilty.

---

[6]   CNN: Report" Richard Jewell to get more than $500,000 from NBC, January 3, 1997: web posted at 4:40 p.m. EST.

In 1996, then president of CNN News stated, "I know at CNN, more care will be taken through the entire process." He feels CNN's reporting on the Jewell story was "accurate and fair," but acknowledges the tremendous pressures of deadlines and competition and says CNN must work harder not to get caught up in the "frenzy." Johnson says reporters will have to make more of an effort to put sources on the record and to "dig, dig, dig," for the information on the side of the suspect, and that editors have to show greater restraint in deciding where to place the story.[7] And three years later this same network would run another fabricated story titled "Operation Tailwind".

Summers Of The Shark

Look at this as if you were Steven Spielberg or George Lucas directing an up and coming film. Nah, forget Steven, he doesn't want to do any more sequels regarding sharks. The year is 2001 and the news is slow, no big scandals, nothing of doom and gloom to bring to the homes of everyday CCPs, so what happens? A young boy was attacked by a shark at Navarre Beach, Florida. The child is saved by his uncle and flown to the hospital. He survives, barely, but will not live a normal life. Then there is an attack at Daytona Beach, Florida, and then all of the news agencies jump on the bandwagon. 2001 is now known as "THE YEAR OF THE SHARK." There hasn't been this much frenzy about sharks since the book "Jaws" came out. You couldn't turn on the news and not see a story about a shark. You had to feel sorry for the reporters that were stationed in areas that are not near to the oceans. Some of them went to local pet stores seeing if someone had

[7]   Ellen Alderman and Caroline Kennedy, "The legacy of Richard Jewell," Columbia Journalism Review, March/April 1997,

possibly stuck their hand into a tank with a small shark and might have gotten bit. But the news conveniently left out one little tidbit of information. Government records showed that shark attacks in the US were on the decline, and not rising as being shown by news agencies to all of us CCPs.

After the coverage of Enron and World Com ran its course and we knew everything we ever wanted to know about these two companies, it was time to find a new theme to latch onto. Thus we had bestowed on the masses that were glued to the receivers of digitalized truth, "2002 THE SUMMER OF ABDUCTION." With two high profile cases - the two girls in California that were abducted and freed after a shootout with police and suspect, and lest we not forget the Elizabeth Smart case - if you believed the rhetoric sprinklers, every child had a bulls eye painted on their forehead. Once again facts be damned. The unofficial motto of the news agencies is "We have to be the "firstest with the mostest and make sure our ratings are the highest". I know the government is not the most trustworthy organization in the world. But, hey, they wouldn't lie to us would they? However, they do receive a good amount of information from police departments around the country and upon compiling this info they come up with some good statistics. And one of the stats that the news (and I am using that word loosely) organizations forgot to mention was that abductions were down for the year 2002.

Hindsight (or in some cases just dumb asses)

On Sept 11, 2001, I watched in horror as our country was attacked, as did millions of other Americans. While the attack was taking place, President Bush was in Florida meeting with a roomful of children. He was immediately rushed from that location to Air Force One. Once in the air, it was determined that the country was indeed under attack and Air Force One was diverted to a base in Louisiana. This is S.O.P. (Standard Operating Procedure) for the Secret Service, who is the agency that protects the President at all times. Watching the news that night, I saw Peter Jennings keep asking why the President wasn't in DC. It seemed that Peter thought the President was acting in a cowardly manner because he was not availing himself to be a sitting target. Let's take a good look at the situation. Anyone with an IQ larger than their shoe size knows that you do not place the leader of your country in a known location at the beginning of a war. In 2003, we had information saying Saddam would be at a certain palace and we bombed the hell out of it the first night. Guess what? The palace was not the first choice of targets. We heard Saddam might be there and, while I'm writing this, we still have not seen a live broadcast from Saddam. Who knows? We may have got him. So I hope Peter learned a history lesson, such as let the Secret Service and military do the jobs they are trained for and you just sit there and look pretty. Please don't think I am picking on Peter only. Dan Rather and Tom Brokaw are guilty of the same diarrhea of the mouth that was so prevalent on 9/11.

March 31, 2003

On this day in the war with Iraq, three major events happened and you can judge for yourself if the news agencies are (and I am quoting an ad for ABC News) "No Hype, No Spin and No Fear."

The first one has to do with an interview that NBC/National Geographic reporter, Peter Arnett, gave to the Iraqi news agency in which he said, "Washington's first war plan has just failed because of Iraqi resistance."[8] Later in the interview he stated the information he was giving the American public was fueling the

---

[8]   "Sacked reporter Arnett joins British daily opposed to Iraq war", AFP, Top Stories, March 31, 2003. 1730 Pacific Time.

protesters movement. Arnett went on to state, "I report the truth of what is happening here in Baghdad and will not apologize for it."[9] This is coming from the same mouth that narrated the fraudulent "Tailwind" report for CNN and was fired for that out-and-out fabrication. In the Tailwind production, Arnett stated that the US Army in Viet Nam was using Sarin gas on deserters. This was proven to be a lie and now we are to believe he only tells the truth. But, at last, do not feel sorrow for this geyser of slanted rhetoric for he has landed a job with a tabloid out of London called "The Daily Mirror." This tabloid is one the most liberal medias in the United Kingdom and is vehemently opposed to the war. Now isn't it a surprise that he would join an organization like that. Look at the bright side. If he is working in London, then we're not paying his unemployment and their taxes make ours look real good.

The second has to do with "An ugly incident with a vehicle with women and children involved." This is a direct quote from Mr. Jennings. The on-site reporter called it "a horrible incident" in which seven women and children were killed when they did not stop at a US check point outside of the city of Najaf. The report went on to say the soldiers obeyed the ROEs (Rules of Engagements) in this terrible incident. Okay, here is what was reported by Fox's reporter imbedded with the Army division where the incident took place and at the military briefing. First thing is that there were signs in Arabic stating it was a checkpoint and all vehicles were to stop for inspection. Second, an American service person speaking Arabic was telling everyone to stop for inspection and held up his hand in the universal language that says STOP. Next the military fired warning shots near the vehicle and yet the vehicle kept advancing, then the soldiers shot the engine of the van and that did not deter the driver. Then, as a last stand,

---

[9]   Ibid.

the soldiers shot into the van. Oh I forgot to mention that on Saturday, March 29th, an Iraqi soldier dressed as a cab driver, in a cab that was filled with explosives, drove up to a checkpoint and killed four US servicemen. With that said, the ROEs should read, "If you do not stop the frigging van your ass is going to be considerably heavier due to all the lead in it." I know you think I am showing my Neanderthal side again, but you are wrong. If the Iraqis do not want to play fair in the sandbox, we will make up some rules to get their attention. Their leaders are declaring they have 4,000 martyrs ready for suicide missions, and we have people we are going to protect. At the top of the news program Peter lead into the stories by saying, "The press is fairly limited with all of the information coming out of the war." What damn war is he watching?, because never before in the history of war has there been so much information coming out of a battle the instant it happens, because their reporters are on the scene with the military with satellite phones and unlimited communication hook ups via military communication centers. The buzz-word is the reporters are "imbedded" with certain military units.

The third incident involved an Iraqi woman who was trying to cross a bridge in Najaf. She was trying to escape from the local military and was on foot when she was shot in the back and her body was thrown into the river. This story never made in into the "Prime Time News" because it did not show the US troops in a bad light. This information came out of a military briefing given by Brig. General Vincent Brooks, and at the end of the meeting, General Brooks stated "The lady's body was recovered by US troops and given to her family for proper burial."

BIAS

On February 12, 1996, Bernard Goldberg committed the unpardonable sin. Mr. Goldberg wrote an op-ed piece for The

Wall Street Journal describing the liberal bias in the media. Mr. Goldberg would have been forgiven for slapping Billy Graham, kicking the Pope, or even eating a ham sandwich, but he attacked the "News Mafia."[10] Mr. Goldberg knows of what he writes since he spent half of his adult life working for CBS, approximately 28 years, until he was fired. He is about as far from a right wing whacko as you can get. The following is a description of himself:

"My parents had to cash in a small insurance policy to get me started in college, another public school, Rutgers University in New Brunswick, New Jersey. At Rutgers, like most of us on campus in the 1960s, I was liberal on all the big issues. I was an especially big fan of Lyndon Johnson's Great Society. I thought then, and still do today, that Martin Luther King is one of the two or three greatest and most courageous Americans of the Twentieth century. I didn't vote for Reagan either time. But I did vote for McGovern twice once in the Florida primary and again in the 1972 general election. I'm pro-choice, with reservations, especially when it comes to minors. And I am for gay rights, too. Not exactly the credentials of some raging right-winger or even some country club Republican. By way of full disclosure, I admit I had a flirtation with conservatism in my younger days. When I was a little kid growing up in the Bronx in the 1950s, I was a die-hard Yankee fan, but I swear that's the closest I've ever come to openly supporting the military-industrial complex or anything so blatantly right-wing."[11]

After the op-ed came out, all hell broke loose for Mr. Goldberg. His associates at CBS treated him as if he had

---

[10] Bernard Goldberg, <u>Bias: A CBS Insider Exposes How the Media Distort the News</u> (Perennial 2002), 16.

[11] Bernard Goldberg, <u>Bias: A CBS Insider Exposes How the Media Distort the News</u> (Perennial 2002), 55-56

done a piece on Three Mile Island and had not used protective clothing, thus making him too hot to handle. He received letters from all sorts of CCPs, some in his industry, the majority not very nice, and these are supposed to be professional reporters; and the ones supporting him would not do it in public. We all know what the term "Political Suicide" means. Then he received a letter from a CCP by the name of Herbert Russell of Carbondale, Illinois, that stated, "Liberal bias among television networks has done something that market forces could not have engendered, the revitalization of radio. Rush Limbaugh would never have become the success he is, if the firm of Rather, Brokaw, and Jennings had done its job. Instead, they failed." [12]

Mr. Russell hit the nail on the head with a pile driver; if you listen to talk radio today, 90% of the programs are hard-core conservative. This is truly a messed up world we live in when the video programs are liberal and the audio programs are conservative. Does that mean all of us moderates have to turn on the television and mute the sound and then turn on the radio and maybe the truth will blend together with the two medias in the Ethernet somewhere and the truth will then fall to earth like rain? Excuse me if I don't hold my breath waiting for this to happen. I have a hard time listening to Rush Limbaugh just because of the opening lines of his program where he is bragging about a brain given from God. My father taught me a lesson when I was young and it is obvious Rush was running his mouth when his daddy was trying to tell him this. "When you are good you won't have to tell anyone you are good, they will know it."

I am not saying that people in the media are not fair, but they are definitely the minority (maybe that is how they got the job - "Affirmative Action". Stupid me; moderates or

---

[12] Ibid. 51.

conservatives are not the correct type of minority). A good example is John Stossel of ABC. He is famous for his line "Give me a Break." Hang in there, John. All of us CCPs are rooting for you.

"During the Clinton impeachment trial in 1999, as the senators signed their names in the oath book, swearing they would be fair and impartial, Peter Jennings, who was anchoring ABC News's live coverage, made sure his audience knew which senators were conservative, but uttered not a word about which ones were liberal. As the senators each signed the oath book, Jennings identified several Democrats, including Barbara Boxer and Ted Kennedy, two of the most liberal members of the Senate, without ever mentioning that they are indeed liberal. That would have been just fine, except for what happened later. When Senator John McCain signed the book, Jennings said, Senator John McCain here of Arizona, left-hander. More right than left in his politics and intending to run for the president of the United States."[13]

As stated earlier, every time a Senator that was not liberal signed the book, Jennings took it upon himself to be sure to point out to the public that these bodies signing the books were conservatives. Do conservatives have a contagious disease? Have these people been abducted by aliens? And is this just a shell of their former selves we are seeing? Or does Jennings want you to look closely at the wanted poster at the post office and see if any of these people's pictures are there? Maybe he is trying to get a new program on the air, something like "America's Most Wanted, Find The Conservative." "There's a better chance that Peter Jennings, the cool, sophisticated Canadian, would identify Mother Teresa as 'the old broad who

---

[13] Ibid. 63-64.

used to work in India' than there is that he would call a liberal Democrat . . . a liberal Democrat!"[14]

"In the world of the Jenningses and Brokaws and Rathers, conservatives are out of the mainstream and need to be identified. Liberals, on the other hand, are the mainstream and don't need to be identified."[15]

I am not saying that the new kids on the block, Fox News Channel, are the great, one size fits all folks on their views of the status of the world. Anyone watching knows they are closer to the right than the left and they do have some true liberals working for them, but they are at least willing to have a dialogue with both sides of an issue. Yes, it is true the news personality can become rude, loud and generally obnoxious if the person being interviewed doesn't agree with the Fox anchor, but then again, if you do not agree with my point of view, to hell with you!

---

[14] Ibid. 64.

[15] Ibid. 65

5.   HUMOR

"If a man takes a long hard look at his life before he dies and can make the following statement, then he has truly had a good life. If he has had one good woman, one good dog and one good friend, that man has had a blessed life." - Dexter Lloyd Cotton, my father.

This statement could be modified to be PC, but since we all know I am a PC caveman (notice the word "man"), I am not about to change it. So therefore, relying on that statement, I can say that I am truly a blessed man, but I will amend the statement to fit my position in life. I have two good women in my life, my wife, Jeannie, and my daughter, Jeneva. Regarding dogs, I have had a number of them, Dee Dee, Goldie, Pebbles, Smokie, and D. D. (aka Damnit Dog). Friends, what can you say, you cannot have enough of them. This chapter does not come from my warped brain. All of these jokes come from so-called friends of mine and, trust me, some of these people are sicker than I am.

This first form of twisted humor comes from Gary Jernigan of Pensacola, FL and his CCP number is 69. Gary, you can thank "Rabbit" for the number. As Gary stated in his e-mail, "If you can read this story without tears of laughter running down your cheeks, then truly there is no hope for you!"

The Chili Cook-Off Contest

*Note: Please take the time to read this slowly. If you pay attention to the first two judges, the reaction of the third judge is even better. For those of you who have lived in Texas, you know how true this is. They actually have a Chili Cook-off about the time the Rodeo comes to town in Houston. It takes up a major portion of the parking lot at the Astrodome. The notes are from an inexperienced Chili taster named Frank, who was visiting Texas from the East Coast.

Frank: "Recently, I was honored to be selected as a judge at a chili cook-off. Judge #3 called in sick at the last moment and I happened to be standing there at the judge's table asking for directions to the Budweiser truck, when the call came in. I was assured by the other two judges (Native Texans) that the chili wouldn't be all that spicy and, besides, they told me I could have free beer during the tasting, so I accepted."

Here are the scorecards from the event:

Chili #1 Mike's Maniac Mobster Monster

Judge #1: A little too heavy on the tomato. Amusing kick.
Judge #2: Nice, smooth tomato flavor. Very mild!
Frank: Holy shit, what the hell is this stuff? You could remove dried paint from your driveway. Took me two beers to put the flames out. I hope that's the worst one. These Texans are crazy.

Chili #2 Arthur's Afterburner

Judge #1: Smoky, with a hint of pork. Slight Jalapeno tang.

Judge #2: Exciting BBQ flavor, needs more peppers to be taken seriously.

Frank: Keep this out of the reach of children. I'm not sure what I'm supposed to taste besides pain. I had to wave off two people who wanted to give me the Heimlich maneuver. They had to rush in more beer when they saw the look on my face.

Chili #3: Fred's Famous Burn Down the Barn

Judge #1: Excellent firehouse chili. Great Kick. Needs more beans.

Judge #2: A beanless chili, a bit salty, good use of peppers.

Frank: Call the EPA. I've located a uranium spill. My nose feels like I have been snorting Drano. Everyone knows the routine by now. Get me more beer before I ignite. The barmaid pounded me on the back, now my backbone is in the front part of my chest. I'm getting shit-faced from all of the beer.

Chili #4: Bubba's Black Magic

Judge #1: Black bean chili with almost no spice. Disappointing.

Judge #2: Hint of lime, good side dish for fish or other mild foods, not much of a chili.

Frank: I felt something scraping across my tongue, but was unable to taste it. Is it possible to burn out taste buds? Sally, the barmaid, was standing behind me with fresh refills. That 300-lb bitch is starting to look HOT. Just like this nuclear waste I'm eating. Is chili an aphrodisiac?

Chili #5 Linda's Legal Lip Remover

Judge #1: Meaty strong chili. Cayenne peppers freshly ground, adding considerable kick. Very impressive!

Judge #2: Chili using shredded beef could use more tomato. Must admit the cayenne peppers make a strong statement.

Frank: My ears are ringing, sweat is pouring off my forehead and I can no longer focus my eyes. I farted and four people behind me needed paramedics. The contestant seemed offended when I told her that her chili had given me brain damage. Sally saved my tongue from bleeding by pouring beer directly on it from the pitcher. I wonder if I'm burning my lips off. It really pisses me off that the other judges asked me to stop screaming. Screw those rednecks.

Chili #6 Vera's Very Vegetarian Variety

Judge #1: Thin yet bold vegetarian variety chili. Good balance of spices and peppers.

Judge #2: The best yet, aggressive use of peppers, onions and garlic. Superb.

Frank: I crapped on myself when I farted and I'm worried it will eat through the chair. No one seems inclined to stand behind me except that slut Sally. She must be kinkier than I thought. Can't feel my lips anymore. I need to wipe my ass with a snow cone.

Chili #7 Susan's Screaming Sensation

Judge #1: A mediocre chili with too much reliance on canned peppers.

Judge #2: Ho hum, tastes as if the chef literally threw in a can of chili peppers at the last moment. I should take note that I am worried about Judge #3 (Frank). He appears to be in a bit of distress as he is cursing uncontrollably.

Frank: You could put a grenade in my mouth, pull the pin, and I wouldn't feel a thing. I've lost sight in one eye, and the world sounds like it is made of rushing water. My shirt is covered with chili, which slid unnoticed out of my mouth. My pants are full of lava-like crap to match my shirt. At least during the autopsy, they'll know what killed me. I've decided to stop breathing it's too painful. Screw it; I'm not getting any oxygen anyway. If I need air, I'll just suck it in through the 4-inch hole in my stomach.

Chili #8 Tommy's Toenail Curling Chili

Judge #1: The perfect ending, this is a nice blend chili. Not too bold but spicy enough to declare its existence.

Judge #2: This final entry is a good balanced chili. This is neither mild nor hot. Sorry to see that most of it was lost when Judge #3 passed out, fell over and pulled the chili pot down on top of himself. Not sure if he's going to make it. Poor dude, wonder how he'd have reacted to really hot chili?

The next bit of humor comes from Nick Carter also from P'cola and his CCP number is 100. Nick is retired from the Air Force and flew in KC-135's most of his career, but I am sure he was on the ark with Noah ensuring the load would stay balanced.

Work Evaluations

These quotes were taken from performance evaluations.

1. "Since my last report, this employee has reached rock bottom and has started to dig."
2. "I would not allow this employee to breed."
3. "This associate is really not so much of a has-been, but more of a definitely won't be."
4. "This young lady has delusions of adequacy."
5. "Works well when under constant supervision and cornered like a rat in a trap."
6. "When she opened her mouth, it seems that this is only to change whichever foot was previously in there."
7. "He sets low personal standards and then consistently fails to achieve them."
8. "This employee is depriving a village of an idiot."
9. "This employee should go far and the sooner he starts, the better."

These are from military performance appraisals.

1. "Got into the gene pool while the lifeguard wasn't watching".
2. "A room temperature IQ."
3. "Got a full 6-pack, but lacks the plastic thingy to hold it all together."
4. "A gross ignoramus, that's 144 times worse than an ordinary ignoramus."

5. "A photographic memory but with the lens cover glued on."
6. "Bright as Alaska in December."
7. "Gates are down, the lights are flashing, but the train isn't coming."
8. "He's so dense, light bends around him."
9. "If he were any more stupid, he'd have to be watered twice a week."
10. "It's hard to believe that he beat out 1,000,000 other sperm."

These next two were sent to me from Ross Atkins of Gulf Breeze, FL and his CCP number is 89 since he is still trying to break 90 on the golf course. Ross, Jeannie said she would get you back for these lawyer jokes.

Lawyers

1. The Post Office just recalled their latest stamps. They had pictures of lawyers on them and people couldn't figure out which side to spit on.
2. How can a pregnant woman tell that she's carrying a future lawyer? She has an uncontrollable craving for baloney.
3. How does an attorney sleep? First he lies on one side, and then he lies on the other.
4. How many lawyer jokes are there? Only three, the rest are true stories.
5. How many lawyers does it take to change a light bulb? How many can you afford?
6. What is the difference between a leech and a lawyer? When you die, a leech lets go.
7. If a lawyer and an IRS agent were both drowning,

and you could save only one of them, would you go to lunch or read the paper?

8. What did the lawyer name his daughter? Sue.

9. What do you call 25 skydiving lawyers? Skeet.

10. What do you call a lawyer that has gone bad? Senator.

11. What do you call a lawyer with an IQ of 50? Your honor.

12. What do you throw to a drowning lawyer? His partners.

13. What does a lawyer use for birth control? His personality.

14. What happens when you cross a pig with a lawyer? Nothing, there are some things a pig won't do.

15. What's the difference between a lawyer and a vulture? The lawyer gets frequent flyer miles.

16. What's another difference between a lawyer and a vulture? Removable wing tips.

17. What's a crying shame? Seeing a busload of lawyers going over a cliff and spotting an empty seat.

18. Why have you never heard of a shark attack against a lawyer? Professional courtesy.

Grandfather, Son, Grandson

A father, son and grandson go out to the country club for their weekly round of golf. Just as they reach the first tee, a beautiful young blonde woman carrying her bag of clubs approaches them. She explains that the member who brought her to the club for a round of golf had an emergency, which called him away and asks the trio whether she can join them.

Naturally, the guys all agree. Smiling, the blonde thanks them and says, "Look, fellows, I work in a topless bar as a dancer, so nothing shocks me anymore. If any of you wants to smoke cigars, have a beer, bet, swear or tell off-color stories or do anything that you normally do when playing a round together, go ahead. But I enjoy playing golf, consider myself pretty good at it, so don't try to coach me on how to play my shots."

With that the guys agree to relax and invite her to drive first. All eyes are fastened on her shapely behind as she bends to place her ball on the tee. She then takes her driver and hits the ball 270 yards down the middle, right in front of the green. The father's mouth is agape.

"That was beautiful," said the dad. The blonde puts her driver away and says, "I really didn't get into it and I should have faded it a little." After the three guys hit their drives and their second shots (she was closest to the pin) the blonde takes out a nine iron and lofts the ball within five feet of the hole. The son says, "Damn lady, you played that perfectly."

The blonde frowns and says, "It was a little weak. I've left a tricky little putt." After the son buries a long putt for a par, dad two putts for a bogey and granddad overruns the green with his pitching wedge, chips back and putts for a double bogey, the blonde taps in the five-footer for a birdie.

The guys all congratulate her on her fine game. She puts her putter back in the bag and says, "Thanks, but I really haven't played much lately, and I'm a little rusty. Maybe I'll really get into this next drive." Having the honors, she drives first on the second hole and knocks the hell out of the ball, and it lands nearly 300 yards away smack in the middle of the fairway. For the rest of the round the statuesque blonde continues to amaze the guys, quietly and methodically shooting for par or less on every hole.

When they get to the 18th green, the blonde is three under par, but has a very nasty 12-foot putt on an undulating green for a par. She turns to the three guys and says, "I really want to thank you all for not acting like a bunch of chauvinists and telling me what club to use or how to play a shot, but I need this putt for a 69 and I'd really like to break 70 on this course. If any one of you can tell me how to make par on this hole, I'll take him back to my apartment, pour some 25-year old Royal Salute Scotch in him, fix him dinner and then show him a good time the rest of the night."

The yuppie grandson jumps at the thought. He strolls across the green, carefully eyes the line of the putt and finally says, "Honey, aim about six inches to the right of the hole and hit it firm. It will get over that little hump and break right into the cup."

The father kneels down and sights the putt using his putter as a plumb bob. "Don't listen to the kid, darlin', you want to hit it softly ten inches to the right and run it left down that little hogback, so it falls into the cup."

The old gray haired grandfather walks over to the blonde's ball on the green, picks it up and hands it to her. "That's a gimme, sweetheart your car or mine?"

This one comes from my daughter. Her CCP number is 111. We sent her to college, hoping she would become one of the pillars of the community and what did we end up with? Someone that is just as sick as her mother and father. I guess that old saying, "the apple does not fall from the tree" is very true.

Edible Words or Statements

Have you ever spoken and wished that you could take the words back or that you could crawl into a hole? Here are a few people who do.

1. I walked into a hair salon with my husband and three kids in tow and asked loudly, "How much do

you charge for a shampoo and a blow job?" I turned around and walked back out and never went back. My husband didn't say a word, he knew better. **Melinda, 39, Sequin, TX.**

2. I was at the golf store comparing the different kinds of golf balls. I was unhappy with the women's type I had been using. After browsing for several minutes, I was approached by one of the good-looking gentlemen who worked at the store. He asked if he could help me. Without thinking, I looked at him and said, "I think I like playing with men's balls." **Colleen, 31, Ferndale, MI.**

3. My sister and I were at the mall and passed by a store that sold a variety of nuts. As we were looking at the display case, the boy behind the counter asked if we needed any help. I replied, "No, I'm just looking at your nuts." My sister started to laugh hysterically, the boy grinned, and I turned beet-red and walked away. To this day, my sister has never let me forget. **Faye, 34, Ellerslie, MD.**

4. While in line at the bank one afternoon, my toddler decided to release some pent-up energy and ran amok. I was finally able to grab hold of her after receiving looks of disgust and annoyance from other patrons. I told her that if she did not start behaving "right now" she would be punished. To my horror, she looked me in the eye and said in a voice just as threatening, "If you don't let me go right now, I will tell Grandma that I saw you kissing Daddy's pee-pee last night!" The silence was deafening after this enlightening exchange. Even the tellers stopped what they doing. I mustered up the last of my dignity and walked out of the bank with my daughter in tow.

The last thing I heard when the door closed behind me was screams of laughter. **Amy, Stafford, VA.**

5. A lady picked up several items at a discount store. When she finally got up to the checker, she learned that one of her items had no price tag. Imagine her embarrassment when the checker got on the intercom and boomed out for all of the store to hear, "Price check on lane thirteen, Tampax super size." That was bad enough, but somebody at the rear of the store apparently misunderstood the word "Tampax" for "Thumbtacks." In a business-like tone, a voice boomed back over the intercom, "Do you want the kind you push in with your thumb or the kind you pound in with a hammer?" **Diane.**

6. Have you ever asked your child a question too many times? My three-year-old son had a lot of problems with potty training and I was on him constantly. One day we stopped at Taco Bell for a quick lunch in between errands. It was very busy, with a full dining room. While enjoying my taco, I smelled something funny, so of course I checked my seven-month-old daughter and she was clean. Then I realized that Danny had not asked to go potty in a while, so I asked him if he needed to go, and he said "No." I kept thinking, "Oh Lord, that child has had an accident, and I don't have any clothes with me." Then I said, "Danny, are you SURE you didn't have an accident?" "No," he replied. I just KNEW that he must have had an accident, because the smell was getting worse. Soooooo! I asked one more time, "Danny, did you have an accident?" This time he jumped up, yanked down his pants, bent over and spread his cheeks and yelled. "SEE MOM, ITS' JUST FARTS!" While thirty people nearly choked

to death on their tacos laughing, he calmly pulled up his pants and sat down. Just then an elderly couple made me feel better by thanking me for the best laugh they'd ever had! **Anonymous.**

7. This had most of the state of Michigan laughing for 2 days and a very embarrassed female news anchor, who will, in the future, likely think before she speaks. What happened was snow was predicted but none fell. We had a female news anchor that, the day after it was supposed to have snowed and didn't, turned to the weatherman and asked: "So Bob, where's that 8 inches you promised me last night?" Not only did he have to leave the set, but half the crew did too they were laughing so hard. **Denna.**

Gene Grace of St. Cloud, FL, CCP # 1977 (card number coincides with the same year the Tampa Bay Bucs attempted to play football) sent this next one. Gene is originally from North Carolina so he can relate to this.

True Southerners

1. Only a true Southerner knows the difference between a hissie fit and a conniption fit.

2. Nobody but a true Southerner knows how many fish make up a mess.

3. A true Southerner can show or point out to you the general direction of younderways.

4. A true Southerner knows exactly how long "directly" is as in "Going to town, be back directly."

5. Even true Southern babies know that "Gimme some sugar" is not a request for the white, granular sweet substance that sits in a pretty little bowl in the middle of the table.

6. All true Southerners know exactly when "by and by" is.

7. True Southerners know instinctively that the best gesture of solace for a neighbor who's got trouble is a plate of hot fried chicken and a big bowl of cold tater salad. (If the trouble is a real crisis, they also know to add some hot biscuits and nanner puddin.)

8. True Southerners grow up knowing the difference between "pert near" and "a right fur piece."

9. True Southerners both know and understand the differences between a redneck, a good ol' boy, and po' white trash.

10. No true Southerner would ever assume that the car with the flashing turn signal is actually going to make a turn.

11. True Southerners know that "fixin" can be used as a noun, verb and adverb.

12. True Southerners have always known how far a "Right Smart" is. Or how big or how much it is.

My stepson Kevin Luddy, CCP # 777 of Las Vegas, NV sent me this next bit of wisdom. Once again it shows males cannot think with their head and cranium at the same time

Condoms

My girlfriend and I were dating for over a year, and so we decided to get married. My parents helped us in every way, my friends encouraged me, and my girlfriend? She was a dream.

There was only one thing bothering me, quite much indeed, and that was my mother-in-law to be. She was a career woman, smart, but most of all beautiful and sexy, who sometimes flirted with me, which made me feel uncomfortable. One day she called me and asked me to come over to check the wedding invitations. So I went. She was alone, and when I arrived, she whispered to me that soon I was to be married, and she had feelings and desires for me that she couldn't overcome. So before I got married and committed my life to her daughter, she wanted to make love to me just once. What could I say? I was in total shock, and couldn't say a word. So, she said, "I'll go to the bedroom, and if you are up to it, just come and get me!" I stood there for a moment, and then turned around and went to the front door. I opened it, and stepped out of the house.

Her husband was standing outside, and with tears in his eyes, hugged me

And then said, "We are very happy and pleased you have passed our little test. We couldn't have asked for a better man for our daughter. Welcome to the family."

Moral of the story:
Always keep your condoms in your car!

John Powers of Snohomish, WA, CCP# 2000 (Y2K has come back to haunt you, John) may have sent a true statement to us instead of a joke.

Surgeons After Work Drinks

The first surgeon says, "I like to see accountants on my operating table, because when you open them up, everything inside is numbered."

The second surgeon responds, "Yeah but you should try electricians! Everything inside them is color coded."

The third surgeon says, "No, I really think librarians are the best; everything inside them is in alphabetical order."

The fourth surgeon chimes in: "You know, I like construction workers, those guys always understand when you have a few parts left over at the end, and when the job takes longer than you said it would."

But the fifth surgeon shut them all up when he observed: "You're all wrong. Politicians are the easiest to operate on. They have no guts, no heart, no balls, no brains and no spine, and the head and the ass are interchangeable.

That last surgeon must have operated on the majority of Congress.

My brother Rick Cotton who lives in Pensacola, FL, CCP #2 (he is #2 in birth ranking and he also follows me in the looks and brains department!) sent this statement to me.

George Carlin On Being An American

I am your worst nightmare. I am a BAD American. I am George Carlin.

1. I like big cars, big hooters, and big paychecks.
2. I believe the money I make belongs to me and my family, not some mid level governmental functionary with a bad comb-over who wants to give it away to crack addicts squirting out babies.
3. I'm not in touch with my feelings and I like it that way. Damn it!
4. I think owning a gun doesn't make you a killer, it makes you a smart American.
5. I think being a minority does not make you noble or victimized, and does not entitle you to anything.
6. I believe that if you are selling me a Big Mac, you better do it in English.
7. I think fireworks should be legal on the 4th of July.
8. I think that being a student doesn't give you any more enlightenment than working at Blockbuster.

In fact, if your parents are footing the bill to put your pansy ass through 4-7 years plus of college, you haven't begun to begin to be enlightened.

9. I believe everyone has a right to pray to his or her God or gods when and where they want to, just leave the rest of us out of it. This also applies to sexuality.

10. My heroes are John Wayne, Babe Ruth, Roy Rogers, and whoever canceled Dr. Quinn Medicine Woman.

11. I don't hate the rich. I don't pity the poor.

12. I know wrestling is a fake and I don't waste any time arguing about it.

13. I think global warming is a big lie. Where are all those experts now, when I'm freezing my ass off during these long winters and paying, paying, paying?

14. I've never owned a slave, or was a slave and I didn't wander forty years in the desert after getting chased out of Egypt. I haven't burned any witches or been persecuted by the Turks and neither have you! So, shut-the-Hell-up already.

15. I want to know which church is it exactly where the Reverend Jesse Jackson practices, where he gets his money, and why he is always part of the problem and not the solution. Can I get an AMEN on that one?

16. I think the cops have every right to shoot your sorry ass if you're running from them.

17. I also think they have the right to pull your ass over if you're breaking the law, regardless of what color you are.

18. I think if you are too stupid to know how a ballot works, I don't want you deciding who should be

running the most powerful nation in the world for the next four years.

19. I dislike those people standing in the intersections trying to sell me crap or trying to guilt me into making "donations" to their cause. These people should be targets.

20. I think if you are in the passing lane, and not passing, your license should be revoked, and you should be forced to ride the bus for at least 2 years and promise never to delay the rest of us ever again.

21. I think Dr. Seuss was a genius.

22. I am neither angry, nor disenfranchised, no matter how desperately the mainstream media would like the world to believe otherwise.

23. I think beef jerky could quite possibly be the perfect food.

24. I think tattoos and piercings are fine if you want them, but please don't pretend that they are a "political statement".

25. I believe it's called the "Boy Scouts of America" for a reason.

26. I don't use the excuse "It's for the children" as a shield for unpopular opinions or actions.

27. I believe that it doesn't take a village to raise a child. It takes two parents.

28. I believe if she has her lips on your Willie, its sex, and this applies even if you are President of the United States.

29. And what the hell is going on with the gas prices, again.

If all of this makes me a BAD American, then yes, I'm a BAD American.

Al Brasher lives in Olympia, WA, CCP# 6969BC (year of birth and CCP # are the same). Al is so old the world had not developed a written language thus no birth certificate. And rumor has it he was the brew master on Noah's Ark (plus he is a rabid Alabama fan and numbers scare them. Ask their last football coach who didn't sign his $10 million contract). He sent me the following two statements and the first one is from some outhouse satirist, who definitely stole some ideas from George Carlin. For all of you that are thinking I am only selecting jokes from my friends that lean to the right, the following two are from a fellow that not only lives on the "Left Coast" but is also a "Lefty" when it comes to politics. After you read these you will swear that I am lying, but trust me, he is a card carrying Democrat.

I.

1. I like big cars, big boats, big motorcycles, big houses and big campfires.
2. I believe the money I make belongs to me and my family, and not some government stooge who wants to give it away to crack addicts.
3. Guns do not make you a killer. I think killing makes you a killer. You can kill someone with a baseball or a car, but no one is trying to ban you from driving to the ball game.
4. I believe they are called the Boy Scouts for a reason. That is why there are no girls allowed. Girls belong in the GIRL Scouts.
5. I think that if you feel homosexuality is wrong, it is not a phobia, it is an opinion.
6. I don't think being a minority makes you a victim of anything except numbers. The only things I can think of that are truly discriminatory are things

like the United Negro College Fund, Jet Magazine, Black Entertainment Television, The Black Caucus and Miss Black America.

7. Try to have things like the United Caucasian College Fund, Cloud Magazine, White Senators for the Good of America, White Entertainment Television, or Miss White America and see what happens. Jesse Jackson will be knocking down your door.

8. I have the right "NOT" to be tolerant of others because they are different, weird, or tick me off.

9. When 70% of the people who get arrested are black, in cities where 70% of the population is black, that not racial profiling, it is the law of statistics.

10. I know what sex is, and there are not varying degrees of it. If I received sex from one of my subordinates in my office, it wouldn't be a private matter or my personal business. I would be "FIRED" immediately!

11. I believe that if you are selling me a milk shake, a pack of cigarettes, a newspaper or a hotel room, you must do it in English! As a matter of fact, if you want to be an American citizen you should have to speak English! My father and grandfather shouldn't have to die in vain so you can leave the countries you were born in to come over and disrespect ours.

12. I think the police should have every right to shoot your sorry ass if you threaten them after they tell you to stop. If you can't understand the word "freeze" or "stop" in English, see the above lines.

13. I feel much safer letting a machine with no political affiliation recount votes when needed. I know what the definition of lying is.

14. I don't think just because you were not born in this country, you are qualified for any special loan

programs, government sponsored bank loans or tax breaks, etc., so you can open a hotel, coffee shop, trinket store, or any other business. We did not go the aid of certain foreign countries and risk our lives in wars to defend their freedoms so that decades later they could come over here and tell us our constitution is a living document and open to their interpretations.

15. I don't hate the rich. I don't pity the poor. I know wrestling is fake, but so are movies and television, and that doesn't stop you from watching them.

16. I think Bill Gates has every right to keep every penny he made and continue to make more. If it ticks you off, go and invent the next operating system that's better and put your name on the building (or buy an idea for a cheap price and sell it for millions). Ask your buddy that invented the Internet to help you.

17. It doesn't take a whole village to raise a child right, but it does take a parent to stand up to the kid and smack their little asses, when necessary and say NO.

18. I think tattoos and piercings are fine if you want them, but please don't pretend they are a political statement. And please stay home until that new lip ring heals. I don't want to look at your ugly infected mouth as you serve me fries.

19. I am sick of Political Correctness and of all the suck ups that go along with it. I know a lot of black people, and not a single one of them was born in Africa, so how can they be "African-Americans?" Besides, Africa is a continent. I don't go around saying I am a European-American because my great, great, great, great, great grandfather was from Europe. I am proud to be from America and nowhere else.

20. And if you don't like my point of view, tough! That's what FREEDOM is all about. Not political correctness or "entitlement" politics with every little special interest group vying for YOUR tax dollars instead of going where they SHOULD.

The New Constitution

Article I:

You do not have the right to a new car, big screen TV or any other form of wealth. More power to you if you can legally acquire them, but no one is guaranteeing anything.

Article II:

You do not have the right to never be offended. This country is based on freedom, and that means freedom for everyone not just you. You may leave the room, turn the channel, express a different opinion, etc., but the world is full of idiots, and probably always will be, and like the rest of us, you need to simply deal with it.

Article III:

You do not have the right to be free from harm. If you stick a screwdriver in your eye, learn to be more careful; do not expect the tool manufacturer to make you and all your relatives independently wealthy.

Article IV:

You do not have the right to free food and housing. Americans are the most charitable people to be found, and will gladly help anyone in need, but we are quickly growing weary of subsidizing generation after generation of professional useless humans who achieve nothing more than the creation of another generation of professional useless humans.

Article V:

You do not have the right to free health care. That would be nice, but from the looks of public housing, we're just not interested in public health care

Article VI:

You do not have the right to physically harm other people. If you kidnap, rape, intentionally maim, or kill someone, don't be surprised if the rest of us want to see you laying on a table with a needle in your arm.

Article VII:

You do not have the right to the possessions of others. If you rob, cheat or coerce away the goods or services of other citizens, don't be surprised if the rest of us get together and lock you away in a place where you still won't have the right to a big screen color TV, pool tables, weight rooms or a life of leisure.

Article VIII:

You don't have the right to a job. All of us sure want you to have a job, and will gladly help you along in hard times, but we expect you to take advantage of the opportunities of part time jobs, education and vocational training laid before you to make yourself useful.

Article IX:

You do not have the right to happiness. Being an American means that you have the right to PURSUE happiness which by the way, is a lot easier if you are unencumbered by an overabundance of idiotic laws created by those of you who were confused by the Bill of Rights.

Article X:

This is an English speaking country. We don't care where you are from. We welcome you here. English is our language and like the one you left behind, we also have a culture. Learn it or go back to the country and the living conditions you were fleeing.

Ms. Cathy Rupert (Prim and proper, yea right she is a Seahawks fan) of Boise, ID, CCP# 80 (Steve Largents' jersey number) sent this statement to me.

Andy Rooney's Tips For Telemarketers:

Three Little Words That Work!
1.   The three little words are: "Hold On, Please." Saying this, while putting down your phone and walking off (instead of hanging-up immediately) would make each telemarketing call so much more time-consuming that boiler room sales would grind to a halt. Then when you eventually hear the phone company's "beep-beep-beep" tone, you know it's time to go back and hang up your handset, which has efficiently completed its task. These three little words will help eliminate telephone soliciting.

Do you ever get those annoying phone calls with no one on the other end?

2. This is a telemarketing technique where a machine makes phone calls and records the time of day when a person answers the phone. This technique is used to determine the best time of day for a "real" sales person to call back and get someone at home. What you can do after answering, if you notice there is no one there, is to immediately start hitting your # button on the phone, 6 or 7 times, as quickly as possible. This confuses the machine that dialed the call and it kicks your number out of their system.

Another Good Idea:

3. When you get "ads" enclosed with your phone or utility bill, return these "ads" with your payment. Let the sending companies throw their own junk mail away. When you get those "pre-approved" letters in the mail for everything from credit cards to 2nd mortgages and similar type junk, do not throw away the return envelope. Most of these come with postage-paid return envelopes, right? It cost them more than the regular 37 cents postage "IF" and when they receive them back. It costs them nothing if you throw them away! The postage was around 50 cents before the last increase and it is according to the weight. In that case, why not get rid of some of your other junk mail and put it in these cool little, postage-paid return envelopes.

   If you want to remain anonymous, just make sure your name isn't on anything you send them. You can even send the envelope back empty if you want to just to keep them guessing. Eventually, the banks and credit card companies will begin getting their own junk back in the mail. Let's let them know what it's like to get lots of junk mail, and the best of all they're paying for it, twice! Let's help keep our postal service busy since they are saying that e-mail is cutting into their business profits, and that's why they need to increase postage costs again. You get the idea. If enough people follow these tips, it will work.

I remember sitting in my dentist's office (Dr. Crook, I swear that is his real name and he is still practicing in the Brent Building in downtown Pensacola) when I was young and picked up a copy of Readers' Digest. In that magazine there were some sections of humor such as "Laughter is the Best Medicine" and "Humor in Uniform" and I always thought if I wrote a book I would have some areas of humor in it. I have always tried to make people laugh, so I hope you enjoyed this chapter.

6.   COMMERCIALS

*"It has been my experience that folks who have
no vices have very few virtues." . . . . Abraham
Lincoln*

Here is a frightening statistic that I learned on June 19, 2003,
while watching the news. A commercial for the Discovery
Channel educated me and isn't that the purpose of the
Discovery Channel. "The average person spends seven years of
their life watching television so, *Entertain Your Brain*." If the
statistic is true for the average CCP, just think of the wasted
lives that are truly addicted to the "Boob Tube." This brings
a whole new meaning to that other commercial, "A mind is a
terrible thing to waste."

Infomercials

All of us CCPs have channel surfed through these annoying
programs that promise to make you younger, thinner (but not
on top of your head), healthier, hairier, hit the golf ball straighter,
tell your future and let's not forget the most important one,
richer. And, remember the money back guarantees after thirty

days. It is a sure bet that you will have a better chance of seeing a ghost in the Lincoln bedroom when you become the primary resident of the White House (can't wait to see your campaign slogans) than getting all of your money back. Keeping all of these promises in mind, let's follow the golden brick road into the world of infomercials.

Any CCP that has watched two hours of television has seen one of this company's infomercial, RONCO. This company was one of the pioneers in this industry. You know you watched them to see what they have come up with this time. If it wasn't the cute little universal cutter in the jar that was capable of slicing and dicing food or diamonds whichever item you needed chopped, it could do it, then there was the potato cutter that made the perfect French fries, and remember that all time favorite, hair in a can for all of our hair challenged (I usually say bald but the PC Police are in the building) CCPs. The man that owns the company, Ron Popeil, should be pushing Bill Gates as the richest man in the world for all of the different products that he has sold. The sales of the pocket fisherman (a fold up rod & reel) should have been enough to balance the budget of Mexico. He now has a product that is near and dear to my heart (really it is closer to my stomach) and that product is the Showtime Rotisserie & Barbeque Oven. Do not think ill of me brothers and sisters CCPs. I have watched one of these decadent commercials but only after I received one of the ovens for a Christmas present. I will stand before the masses of CCPs and sing Ronco's praises for this product. It actually does everything they say it will do. This is the only one of these wastes of perfectly good air time (true CCPs would rather watch something being blown up or a ball game) that I have watched voluntarily, but to enlighten all of you in the name of research, I will suffer through and watch hours of these programs so that you will have better things to do with your time. Just remember, if you read this chapter, you owe me for the suffering I have endured and trust me I will collect.

Exercise Equipment & Weight Loss

At one time or another you all have seen the ad with the guy with the long hair and a baseball cap, on a machine that looks like a piece of Iraqi torture equipment. He is running on this equipment holding on to the handles and doing splits that most high school cheerleaders would be envious of. The ad is for *Tony Little's Gazelle Fitness Elite.* If you believe everything in this ad, he will guarantee you that he will make every muscle in your body hurt for days after using this machine, while at the incredibly low price of $14.95 per month. And if you will take advantage of the promotion, they will ship it to you for free, which is usually $34.95, what a deal. I still do not know how many months you pay $14.95, the ad never gave a total price, but then again it may and I just missed it while moving my magnifying glass while reading the small print (and do I mean small). If at any time in the first thirty days you do not like the machine send it back for a complete refund of your $14.95. Hell of a deal don't you think, but they will not pay for the return shipping of $34.95. So, any way you look at it, you will be out $20.00. I love the fine print on these ads. You know the ones I am talking about - the before and after pictures. The woman that looks as if she is about to give birth to twins and two months later after using this God-sent machine, you see a photo of her in a bikini looking as if she is competing for the Hawaiian Tropics beauty contest. Or the guy that has a serious case of Dunlap in the before picture and in the after photo, he could go to third world countries and lay by the river and allow the women of the village to use his stomach as a washboard instead of beating the clothes with rocks. The one disclaimer these ads are missing is the name and phone numbers of the plastic surgeons the people used for the butt lifts and tummy tucks. The disclaimer actually says "Not typical results" and another disclaimers states, "Diet and exercise are needed to achieve proper results."

Why is it that everyone that is pictured in this ad has a body fat index of 1%? Why don't they put some fat asses like myself on the screen working up a sweat, isn't that the audience they are marketing to? Look at Tony, the man definitely works out (don't get me wrong I do not walk down that side of the street) and more than thirty minutes every other day to get that shape and that goes for all of the "models" in the ad with him. You and I both know these people have never been to an "All You Can Eat Buffet" and a dessert or beer will never pass their lips. The next question I have is, why is Tony's head always covered? Has anyone ever seen the top of his head? Is he one of those men that have "hat hair?" You do not know what hat hair is? Simply put, the hat covers the place hair used to grow. A good friend of mine named Tom informed me that he was not bald, but that his slick head was a solar panel for a sex machine. Tony, if you are hair-challenged, look at the bright side, as smooth and fast talking a pitchman that you are, maybe you could work up a deal with the Hair Club For Men company, thus splitting the price of your infomercial and you get to test drive one of the hair pieces while exercising on your equipment. The director could go for the close up when the Hair Club portion of the ad was airing regarding wind in the hair look. Just a thought, I am always trying to help companies save expenses thus reducing the price of their product so the savings can be passed on to the CCPs.

Chuck Norris is the spokesperson for *Total Gym* and he obviously uses the machine to do the things he does in movies and TV. I admit I purchased this machine and it will do all of the things they claim it will do. As mentioned earlier I used to play football and in the off season, I was in a gym working out with weights six days a week (no matter how hard I tried I still had "Love Handles"), so I know most of the exercises this machine can do and the ones it will not do. The one draw back to this piece of equipment is that it doesn't have a remote control so I can push a button and have it come out of the closet, set itself up and then eject my ass out of the command module and start the exercise program. Hey Mr. Norris (if you think I am going to call him Chuck, you are crazy), can you get the engineers to work on the remote idea? Just remember, when you buy this equipment, if Chuck ever comes over to your house and sees his equipment gathering dust or rust he is the person that stated in one of his movies "I am going to hit you on the right side of your head so many times you are going to beg for a left" and believe me, he can do it.

The BowFlex is an impressive looking machine and no doubt with all of the resistance you could add to your workout if you were serious about working out. In time you could get the body of the Incredible Hulk or Ms. Hulk, but in reality it will end up in the majority of the CCPs garages collecting dust. But for all of you CCPs who have a contemporary-style home, you could use this piece of equipment as modern art and just think, if you get tired of the way it looks, just rearrange the pulleys to get a new look.

The Magical Pill. I cannot believe how many CCPs fall for this magical elixir that is guaranteed to make you lose weight in your sleep. I would be the first in line to purchase these pills if it would help remove these love handles and deliver that wash board stomach that all of the models have shown in the ads. How many millions of dollars are spent annually for this type of magical product? My poster child for this idea is "The Diet Cookie." Nowhere in my upbringing did I ever see the two words "Diet & Cookie" in the same sentence. And not only have we lived long enough to see this happen, but in its heyday was making a ridiculous amount of money. P. T.

Barnum was correct, "There is a sucker born every minute and two to take him."

Apology

Stick me with a fork I'm done. I know I promised you that I would watch all of the infomercials, but I could not take it any longer. Even the U.S. Constitution has an amendment regarding "Cruel and Unusual Punishment." I know I promised to watch the shows regarding money and how to make you richer. But I am still stuck on the formula on why a person will run for a political office that pays $150,000 per year and spends $20 million of their money to get there. If I can't figure out that simple mathematical formula, how in the world do you expect me to understand all of these high and mighty movers and shakers of the "almighty dollar". There are ads that will teach you how to become a real estate tycoon that would make you Donald Trump's major competitor. Side Note: have you ever noticed how close tycoon and typhoon are in spelling? And in these ads, this is so true again. While promising to make you a tycoon, the pitch that is being delivered by a person is creating enough hot air to spawn a typhoon. Maybe we can get the government agency that name hurricanes and typhoons to start naming these commercials, thus giving the public plenty of warning to seek shelter as in turning the channel.

Not only can you become a real estate typhoon, sorry I meant tycoon, by staying up and watching TV at two in the morning, but you can oversee your vast kingdom of property. Whether it is rental property or one of your many mansions, you will need to survey your vast holding in style. You would not dare show up to your newly purchased castle in a vehicle that looked as if it belonged to Jed Clampett of the "Beverly Hillbillies". That only happens on TV. All you have to do to change your ride is stay up to three a.m. and watch that kid show you how to make your garage look like I-5 in Seattle at rush hour. If you will follow his simple plan, you will own the car of your dream, you will own the car of your neighbor's dream, what the hell, you will own the neighbor's car. This kid looks as if he just got his learner's permit and he is telling us how to wheel and deal in the auto industry. Let's look closer at this kid. Someone told him if you had a Corvette you could get laid. Now you know what his driving force is. More cars, more sex, different cars, more sex. No wonder the kid is so skinny; he is screwing himself to death. If you got to go, there are worse ways of dying.

And let us not forget now that you have become this tycoon. You cannot continue running around acting like the typhoon you are. Stay up to four a.m. and watch the program that will teach you how to reach your inner self. Just below the surface of your skin is a beautiful person looking to escape (for the majority of us, the use of a plastic surgeon is the only way the beautiful person under the skin will come forth, but what the hell, we are all rich, thanks to the infomercials; right?). No longer will you be the A-hole that your friends and enemies think you are, they will look at you in a different light. They will see you as a rich A-hole that has touched his/her inner self (the primary word here is touched).

Now that you have become the rich cosmopolitan person that everyone envies, you now live in the house fit for a king or queen. You have a different royal chariot for every day of the week and, of course you have succeeded in finding inner peace. You have to look the part. This is where the make-up infomercials come into play. In this day of modern science, not only can they bikini wax your entire body, whatever hair is left, the color can be changed. And if you do not have any hair and you truly want said hair, it can be glued in place. There is make-up out there that will lift the eyes, lift the chin, perk up those boobs and lift that drooping ass. In a majority of the asses I've have seen, it would take a front-end loader to accomplish this. All that is required of you is to stay awake until five a.m.

Here is a free piece of advice, for what it is worth: now that you look marvelous, you live in a castle and ride in a car you only see on TV, stand there and look pretty because once you open your mouth your friends and relatives are going to realize you are still the same dumb ass you always were.

Equipment Opportunities

I think the most gullible group of CCPs has to be golfers, although fishermen & hunters are a real close second. Just look at all the new clubs, balls, training aids and God only knows what else. How many times have you seen and heard the promises that this new pitching wedge is going to change your life and guaranteed to get you that "PGA Tour Players Card" that you so desperately want. This club is so good, if your ball lands on a boulder (remember hit 2" behind the ball so you are applying spin), you can blast through this obstacle. If your ball is in 3' of water, it is designed to cut through water at 120 mph, and if you land in a sand bunker, just pick your ball up and add one more stroke to your score because the ball is guaranteed to go in the hole from a bunker. And let's not forget, this club will automatically add spin, forward or reverse, to the ball in such a manner you will swear that it has the same chip in it that a smart bomb has because it will track directly to the hole.

More power. You have to be able to drive the ball at least 350 yards, don't you? These companies are promising you more yardage if you get rid of last years sensation that they sold you and will guarantee this _will_ be the last driver you will ever buy. Didn't they say that last year? Some of these drivers are arriving with weigh restrictions on them. The purpose for this is due to the size of the face of the club. You don't expect some 5' 2" petite female to swing the **Monster Smasher XXXX**. Of course not, her model would be the Monster Smasher X. Now someone my size could handle that XXXX bad boy. These club makers will have you believing that you will have to contact the FAA for clearance every time you pull it out of the bag to tee off. I recently saw an ad for this new driver that was so big, they had to drill holes through the head to allow the air to past through, thus giving you the thrust of jet power. This club comes with a FAA warning for noise abatement. That is, it cannot be used near or in the vicinity of the John Wayne airport, because residents will think it is an airliner taking off. And, of course, there are putters. I could do a whole chapter on these instruments of cruelty alone. One of my favorite ones in the past was made so you could stand it up by itself and then you could walk away to check your alignment. Did they think everyone carried a surveyor's transit in their bag (they do sell laser range finders now) to help align the putt?

The training aids are an industry all in themselves. Some of these devices look as if they came out of the middle ages torture chambers, or at least from Mary Ann's island of pain. One of my favorites is the swing aid that is made of hard plastic or Kevlar, I do not know which, but it looks as if your spouse would have to help you fit into it (corset-looking sucker) then your arms are strapped into these slides. And now you are going to go out in public wearing this equipment. If you wear this while driving to the practice range, will the law still require you to wear a seat belt since it will not fit around you with this equipment on? Once you finished your practice, then you will find out who your true friends are because they are willing to be seen helping you get out of this equipment. Then there is another swing aid that is made out of PVC and is a circle that is approximately 10' in diameter. The good news is when you are finished practicing it doubles as a satellite dish and then you can go inside and watch the "Golf Channel."

And least we not forget the practice clubs. Have you seen the 5 iron that has a hinge in the middle? This will teach you to take the club back slowly and then bring it forward in a controlled manner. I do not know about the people that bought these items, but when I picked one up out of the bags at the golf shops, the head of the club would bend in the middle and hit my hand that was on the grip. I look stupid enough just trying to play golf with regular clubs. I do not need to pay extra money for a club that is going to make me look like a member of the Three Stooges, although that would be a hell of a foursome to watch. If you want to become an instant millionaire, all you have to do is invent a golf training aid with a money-back guarantee; even if you do send the money back, there are enough suckers out there to buy it. You know P. T. Barnum is spinning in his grave, trying to get out to go after these suckers.

FISHERMEN/WOMEN are the next gullible group of people that will buy anything to help them catch that world record fish. I do not believe the women are as gullible as the men since a majority of the time, it is just men being shown in the commercial. The marketing experts are willing to sell these unsuspecting CCPs boats that will get them to that fishing hole at Mach 2. Once they get there, they have sonar that is so accurate they can watch a bass fart. The new rod and reel means there's no need to have the CCPs physically exerting themselves anymore, just push the button and launch the lure into the water in the same manner as the navy use to launched depth charges. Once the lure is in the water it emits an electronic signal that no fish can resist (whether it is a bream or a 25' white shark). Once the elusive fish is hooked on the super duper lure just push the button on the rod and reel and the fish will come at you with the speed of a torpedo launched from a Germany U-Boat. Here comes the physical part. You have to lift the fish out of the water and remove the lure; but rest assured that someone is working on a device that will eliminate you of this disgusting chore. Next, open the lid to the Ice Cooler Model 5000, and place the fish in it, shut the lid and push the button. Just stand back and let the machine work. First it scales the fish, second it guts your little beauty, third it fillets it, then it will vacuum seal the finished product. And finally it is boxed up, with a label and a UPS shipping bar code. Don't worry about contacting UPS; the cooler has made the call and a UPS boat will be by shortly. Do not worry about the waste by-products. Every part of the fish is used. The remaining parts are ground up for fertilizer and shipped to an organic farm. The fishermen of the future's dreams have just come true. Let the equipment do all the work for you so you do not have to interrupt your beer drinking.

My father was into fishing in the later years of his life, and one day I was looking into his tackle box and found a lure that looked like a miniature Budweiser can. Give me a frigging break, how many alcoholic fish are there on this planet? Bear with me on this illustration. Can't you see it now, two bass looking at each other and this "Bud" can comes floating by them. One nudges the other and says "The bar is open and it must be Happy Hour." My father did catch a fish on this lure, but after closer inspection of the fish, he said it looked kind of funny and he would not eat it. Later he told me he caught the fish at the end of a discharge pipe near a nuclear power plant.

Awards

Being a member in good standing of the CCPs and my card number reads number 1, I have created awards for the five best commercials and the five worst commercials (airing at the time this book was being written). The "Golden Remote" will be given to the top five and the "Dead Battery" will go to the worse or dumbest, whichever the case.

Golden Remotes
#1

An ad for California cheese starts out with two cows hunkered down on the floor of the barn and the sunrise is showing through the open barn door. About that time a rooster struts into the barn and begins crowing. One cow looks at the other and says "Do you want to get an early start on the alpha in the lower 40?" The other cow responses "What's the rush, hit the snooze." The next scene you see is the rooster flying out of the barn door, and it hits a #2 wash-tub that is hanging on a fence post, and then hitting the ground. It rises slowly and starts strutting back into the barn.

#2

A USGA (United State Golf Association) commercial starts off showing a young boy (10 to 13 years old) teeing up a golf ball on a par 3 hole. Oh, by the way, he is playing by himself. He takes an iron out of his bag hits the ball and it flies to the green where it hits and rolls into the hole. His eyes get the sizes of saucers, straps on the golf bag and begins walking, which turns into sprinting, to the green. Upon reaching the green he places his bag down and walks up to the hole. He reaches in the hole and pulls out the ball and begins to do a slow turn to see if he can spot a witness. For all of you non-golfers, if you do not have a witness to the hole in one, it is not valid. After completing a 360-degree turn, he comes up empty handed and you see a despondent look on his face. Out of the clear blue sky, a greens keeper drives up on a riding lawn mower and says "Nice hit, kid." As he gets off the lawn mower he says, "You know what this means?" Next scene it is closing time on the golf course and the kid and greens keeper are standing in front of a soda vending machine and the kid answers the previous question. "Drinks are on me." Again for you non-golfers, if you make the elusive hole-in-one, you are supposed to buy everyone that was on the golf course a drink. I hope that last bit of education regarding buying drinks will keep you in the non-golfer category, because the golf gods only allow so many holes in ones and I have not gotten mine yet. After I get mine, feel free to take up golf.

#3

The Kibbles n' Bits dog food commercial that has the dog dancing after the product is poured into the bowl. Everyone has seen dogs dancing for food but when this dog dances, she could hold her own at any dance club. If that was my dog I would definitely sent the video into America's Funniest Video because it would be a sure bet to win the top prize award.

#4

Rental has the next winner… all of the commercials that include the hamster and the rabbit. These ads were first introduced to the public at the Super Bowl. The hamster is always in the thick of things and the rabbit plays the "straight man." It's like watching old Abbott & Costello films. The best one is where the hamster is portraying a martial artist in the pen when he accidentally hits the rabbit with a carrot. The rabbit gets annoyed, snaps his fingers and a dozen "Ninja Mice" appear and begin kicking the hamster's butt.

#5

Coors Beer. The "Wingman." This is one closest to real life than any other commercial shown on TV. Anyone that has dated more than one person has gone out with a friend to cover their "6" by way of running interference so your partner can zoom in on his/her target. Your job is to separate the target's wingman from each other so your partner can make the kill. As you die a slow death listening about his/her life's adventures, the cat, the job and hours of useless chatter. I don't know about the majority of you, but when it was my turn to be the wingman, the deal was "Lead" had to buy the drinks. After six or seven drinks the world definitely looks better, including the person sitting across from you.

The Dead Battery award goes to the stupidest, dumbest, most asinine commercials that have been shown in 2003. These ads are so bad that people who do not even know how to use a remote (at this time of printing there were only five humans in the US that lacked the education to operate a remote) will change channels to keep from subjecting themselves to such misery.

Dead Battery
#1

"Discover To Go Card". Every one of these series of commercials gets this award. The Discover credit card has developed this super-duper little switch blade looking, flip out device that holds the credit card and this little ditty attaches to your key ring. Remember the days you had to worry about the waiter/waitress making a copy of your credit card for personnel use. Now they get a chance to make a copy of your car keys so they can steal it later. One commercial shows an overweight middle-aged man fighting a dozen ninjas with this silly ass card. Another one shows a man whipping out his card, trying to cut a fishing line to save his friend. Even if you used a set of jumper cables on these commercials, they would not be able to add enough power to re-energize these pitiful ads.

#2

"Honey Nut Cheerios" has this clown going around town telling everyone "I've lowered my cholesterol." The only thing I have to say about this dumb ass commercial is "HERE IS A QUARTER (now days it is fifty cents) CALL SOMEONE THAT GIVES A DAMN."

#3

Terminex exterminator's commercials are not even laughable because there are some people out there that would go to that extent to keep bugs away. You have seen the ads where the entire house is made out of concrete because "Hubby" is afraid of termites. #2 a couple is met at the door by the wife wearing shades and the house is lit up enough to land aircraft. "Wifey" then passes the couple a tray with sunshades on it and says "Hubby" is afraid of roaches and the light keeps them away. If the truth was known, the house is really filled with grow lights and it is a marijuana growing operation. #3 "No Bugs" wife opens door, couple is hit with an 80 mph wind that is being generated by huge fans, so spiders and insects can't land, again because "Hubby" is afraid of bugs. First of all, the women should get a divorce from these pansies and in the court documents, part of the agreement should be that these men will attend therapy sessions to overcome their fear of bugs. This will insure if they marry again and have offspring, the male children will not grow up and be the wimp the old man was.

#4

Orbit sugar-free gum ads are glimpses of a little European humor (and I do mean a little, as in microscopic, humor). You always see this perky British female pushing this gum where some poor soul is going to be covered in dirt, mud, or some other form of filth and when all is said and done WHALA, the subject's teeth come out of the incident sparkling clean. Has no one told this bimbo if you keep your mouth shut while you are mud wrestling, it will not get in your mouth thus your teeth are clean. Another one of their stupid ads shows a construction laborer working with a jack hammer as a girl walking her dog passes him by. He smiles at the woman and she slaps him because he was not chewing their gum. Having worked construction for a number of years, I know better than to piss off a laborer with a jack hammer in his hands, much less slap him. Do you catch my drift here? And then the British bimbo appears and says four out of five construction workers use Orbit gum. Miraculously the laborer that got slapped is now chewing the correct gum and the pretty lady walking the dog kisses him. In real life, everyone with an IQ higher than room temperature knows the only thing that dude was chewing was Bull of the Woods or Beechnut chewing tobacco.

#5

Viagra has two commercials that are basically the same. They both are dealing with the man's self-confidence. The first one shows this middle age man coming in to work and he is met inside by a female co-worker where she asks him if he got a haircut. The next person is a male co-worker that asks him if he has lost weight, shaved his moustache, come back from vacation, going on vacation, did he get a promotion, did he get a raise (no, maybe a rise) along with another bunch of asinine questions. The other ad shows a middle age male going into a party and everyone there asks him the same dumb ass questions the group above has already asked. Then he walks up to his wife/significant other and states he went to the doctor and the problem is taken care of.

Now lets look at these two ads as if they were taking place in real life. What looks different about these two guys? Look below the belt, both are supporting "Woody's" so hard a cat could not scratch these weapons. They are walking around like they are fifteen years old again (remember guys when your "Johnson" used to spring into action at the most inappropriate time). They are strutting around like a rooster with pants on. They kind of favor one of those wind vanes you have seen on top of barns. The down side to these two guys is that they are walking around with loaded weapons. You can bet your sweet bibby that if one of their fellow workers dropped anything, they would wait until the smiling pants monster left the building before bending over to pick up the drop item. The guy at the party would have to be careful when he walked into the house and moved throughout the crowd. He could become intimate with a lot of new people or look like a bull in a china shop by knocking over the food dishes and drink glasses with that rejuvenated pointer leading the way. Maybe this drug should come with a warning that after taking and going out in public, a pilot car/person is required.

Lacerated Hair and Screaming

How many CCPs have seen these characters on commercials that are hawking cars, boats, food vacuum sealers, and did I mention cars. You know the ones I am talking about. Not a single hair out of place and has so much Mousse and hair spray in their hair they could walk through a wind tunnel that is producing Mach 2 speed winds and nothing would be blown astray (are these Trent Lott's role models or visa versa). And then to top it off they are screaming so loud that if you hit the mute button you still hear the clown at 50 db. Do these people really think that the average CCP is waiting breathlessly all night to watch these stupid commercials, or are these so called "God's gift to women" with egos so big that they think every living CCP can not wait for their next fix of their stupid commercial? You know, during the Disco, era these yahoos were the ones with all of the gold chains. You have seen these types, the ones that would make Mr. T jealous. Did you ever notice these guys do not get near any body of water? They're not dumb. If they fell in with that much gold, they would never surface.

Most of you will remember the car ad for Isuzu back in the 80s when it featured "Joe Isuzu", the obnoxious lying car salesman. My favorite one was when they had Joe hooked up to a "Lie Detector" and every time he lied, voltage was sent through his body. By the end of the commercial he had enough voltage in his body to light up a small city. Contrary to popular belief, Joe did not start a school for ad "Spokesmen," he was elected to the US House of Representatives. After three terms in the House, he was involved in a scandal regarding checks at the House Post Office, sex with interns and some pictures of animals, whatever that means, and is now residing at Eglin FPC (Federal Prison Camp, Eglin Air Force Base) Ft. Walton, Florida.

Whatever happened to that old law regarding "Truth in Advertising"? Has anyone ever been charged with that archaic law? Is this an oxymoron - truth & advertising? Don't you wish for once that they would not make promises to you, when everyone in the world knows that the product does not have a snow ball's chance in Hades of coming through? Most CCPs would buy the product if the spokesperson said it would last two or three months instead of the life-time warranty it comes with. Then again, it's impossible to get a replacement or your money back if it breaks after you're dead. The following was a story e-mailed to me from my wife, Jean Cotton CCP # 11. I do not know if this story is true, but it is refreshing to think a company rewarded someone for trying to tell the truth in advertising.

Carnation Milk

A little lady from North Carolina had worked in and around family dairy farms since she was old enough to walk, with hours of hard work and little compensation. When canned Carnation Milk became available in the grocery stores (1940s or 1950s), she read an advertisement offering $5,000 for the best slogan, with a rhyme beginning with "Carnation Milk is best of all." She proclaimed, "I know all about milk and dairy farms, I can do this."

She sent in her entry and about a week later, a black limo drove up in the front of her house and a man got out. The man then said, "Carnation LOVED your entry so much, we are here to award you $1,000, even though we will not be able to use it." Here was her entry:

> Carnation milk is best of all.
> No tits to pull, no shit to haul.
> No buckets to wash, no hay to pitch.
> Just poke a hole in the son-of-a-bitch!

NOW WASN'T THAT REFRESHING? FOR ONCE, TRUTH IN ADVERTISING!!

7.   PAST AND PRESENT CCPs

"Some folks are like concrete, all mixed up and permanently set. " ... *A sign on Hwy 12 in Elma, WA.*

Former CCPs

It is sad, but true, that some of our card-carrying members have been nominated, with one of them winning, the annual award, called the Darwin Award. For all of you CCPs that are not familiar with the award, please read the following statement. The award has nothing to with the theory of evolution in relation to the beginning of the world.

Darwin Award *– It's an annual honor given to the person who did the gene pool the biggest service by killing themselves in the most extraordinarily stupid way.*

And the nominees are:

CCP Card # 85423, a young man, searching for a way of getting drunk cheaply, because he had no money with which to buy alcohol, mixed gasoline with milk. Not surprisingly, this concoction made him ill, and he vomited into the fireplace in his house. The resulting explosion and fire burned his house down, killing both him and his sister. This man deprived a village of an idiot.

CCP Card #s 9742354, 257873, 125698, three men were flying in a light aircraft at a low altitude, when another plane approached. It appears that they decided to moon the occupants of the other plane, but lost control of their own aircraft and crashed. They were all found dead in the wreckage with their pants around their ankles. Got a full six-pack but lacked the plastic thingy to hold it all together.

CCP Card #33366, a 27-year-old woman lost control of her car on a highway and crashed into a tree, seriously injuring her passenger and killing herself. As a commonplace road accident, this would not have qualified for a Darwin nomination, were it not for the fact that the driver's attention had been distracted by her Tamagotchi key ring, which had started urgently beeping for food as she drove along. In an attempt to press the correct buttons to save the Tamagotchi's life the woman lost her own. This young lady had delusions of adequacy.

CCP Card #64987, a 22-year-old Reston, VA man was found dead after he tried to use octopus straps to bungee jump off a 70-foot railroad trestle. Fairfax County police said the man, who was a fast-food worker, had taped a bunch of the straps together, and wrapped an end around one foot, anchored the other end to the trestle at Lake Accotink Park, jumped and hit the pavement. A police spokesman, said investigators think the young man was alone because his car was found nearby. "The length of the cord that he had assembled was greater than the distance between the trestle and the ground," the spokesman said, and went on to say the apparent cause of death was "Major trauma." Got into the gene pool while the lifeguard wasn't watching.

CCP Card #79874, a man in Alabama died from rattlesnake bites. It seems that he and a friend were playing a game of catch, using the rattlesnake as a ball. The friend – no doubt a future Darwin Award candidate – was hospitalized. Gates are down, the lights are flashing, but the train isn't coming.

CCP Card #213654, employees in a medium-sized warehouse in west Texas noticed the smell of a gas leak. Sensibly, management evacuated the building extinguishing all potential sources of ignition, lights, power, etc. After the building had been evacuated, two technicians from the gas company were dispatched. Upon entering the building, they found they had a difficult time navigating in the dark. To their frustration, none of the lights worked. Witness later described the sight of one of the technicians reaching into his pocket and retrieving an object that resembled a cigarette lighter. Upon operation of the lighter like object, the gas in the warehouse exploded, sending pieces of it up to three miles away. Nothing was found of the technicians, but the lighter was virtually untouched by the explosion. The technician that was suspected of causing the blast had never been thought of as "bright" by his peers. It's hard to believe that this man beat out 1,000,000 other sperm.

And The Winner

CCP Card #753159, the Arizona Highway Patrol came upon a pile of smoldering metal embedded into the side of a cliff rising above the road at the apex of a curve. The wreckage resembled the site of an airplane crash, but it was a car. The car was unidentifiable at the scene. The lab finally figured out what it was and what had happened. It seems that a guy had somehow gotten hold of a JATO (Jet Assisted Take Off, actually a solid fuel rocket) unit that is used to give heavy military transport planes an extra "push" for taking off from short airfields. He had driven his Chevy Impala out into the desert and found a long and straight stretch of road. Then he attached the JATO unit to his car jumped in, got up some speed and fired off the JATO! The facts as best as could be determined are that the operator of the 1967 impala hit the JATO ignition at a distance of approximately 3.0 miles from the crash site. This theory was established by the prominent scorched and melted asphalt on the road at that location. The JATO, if operating properly, would have reached maximum thrust within 5 seconds, causing the Chevy to reach speeds well in excess of 350 mph and continuing at full power for an additional 20-25 seconds. The driver, and soon to be pilot, most likely could have experience G-forces usually reserved for fighter pilots under full afterburner, causing him to become insignificant for the remainder of the event. However, the automobile remained on the straight highway for about 2.5 miles (15-20 seconds) before the driver applied and completely melted the brakes, blowing the tires and leaving thick rubber marks on the road surface, then becoming airborne for an additional 1.4 miles and impacting the cliff face at a height of 125 feet leaving a blackened crater 3 feet deep in the rock. Most of the driver's remains were not recoverable; however small fragments of bone, teeth and hair were extracted from the crater and fingernail and bone shards were removed from a piece of debris believed to be a portion of the steering wheel. It has been calculated that this moron nearly reached Mach 1, attaining a ground speed of approximately 420 mph. This man was so dense, light would bend around him.

The "This Person Should Not Be Allow To Breed" Award

CCP Card #65428, based on a bet by the other members of his threesome, tried to wash his own "balls" in a ball washer at the local golf course. Proving once again that beer and testosterone are a bad mix, 65428 managed to straddle the ball washer and dangle his scrotum in the machine. Much to his dismay, one of his buddies upped the ante by spinning the crank on the machine with 65428's scrotum in place, thus wedging them solidly in the mechanism. 65428, who immediately passed his threshold of pain, collapsed and tumbled from his perch. Unfortunately for 65428, the height of the ball washer was more than a foot higher off the ground than his testicles are in a normal stance, and the scrotum was the weakest link. 65428's scrotum was ripped open during the fall, and one testicle was plucked from him forever and remained in the ball washer, while the other testicle was compressed and flattened as it was pulled between the housing of the washer and the rotating machinery inside. To add insult to injury, 65428 broke a new $300 driver that he had just purchased from the pro shop, and was using it to balance himself. 65428, was rushed to the hospital for surgery, and the remaining threesome were asked to leave the course.

Present CCPs

Arnold Schwarzenegger

That last name not only sends chills up and down the spine of his enemies in the movies, but it just made my spell checker commit suicide. CCP # T3, rendition of General MacAuthor's "I shall return" is truly unique. Never in my wildest dreams did I think anyone could take a statement that short and make it so powerful, as well as profitable. What true CCP could forget those immortal words "I'll be back!" Early, in his career, Mr. S. (the computer was just revived and I don't want to chance another crash and I do not want to offend T3. New computer I can buy, new body is not optional), said those words. Hollywood did not know how true those words were.

"Arnold is remembering back to where his journey began, back to Austria, back to where he grew up, in the tiny hamlet of Thal-by-Graz. 'I was a farm boy from out in the village. We had no TV. No electricity. No refrigerator. No flushing toilets. We had nothing in the house. Absolutely nothing. But I never felt I was poor as a kid. I'd see my mother make a sweater and my father make a little figure with his knife. And that was a Christmas gift. We were delighted with those things and I didn't feel I was cheated out of anything – or that it would hold me back.' Out of his childhood, Arnold says, came a lesson that would guide him for the rest of his life: **"Don't worry about where you come from. Worry more about where you are going.**"[16]

Arnold did something the majority of people refused to do, and that was work hard and long to make his dreams come true. No one gave him anything all. Those hours he spent lifting weights were his ticket out of that little town and it was not wasted on just buying the ticket. I'm sure it helped him in getting laid on a regular basis. Trust me you don't want a male CCP that big walking around with pent-up frustration. You do not know what he would do or to who. Trust me, I am not saying Arnold walks (or walked) down that side of the street when he was younger but to play it safe, if I had dropped my wallet in front of him I would have kicked it back to the car before I bent over to pick it up. Arnold was the butt end of jokes when he first came to Hollywood. The stereotypical jock, all muscle and no brains, and everyone (except me, just in case he reads the book) made fun of his accent. So, did Arnold throw up his hands and cry, "Why Me?", and then start screaming for the government to give him his fair share?

No, he started taking acting classes and voice lessons (Note to Arnold: please give me the name of your voice instructor, maybe he can help me with my Southern Drawl). Arnold, along with Arnold Inc., was successful in getting passed on the California ballot an initiative known as Proposition 49. "This initiative allows the use of public schools, K through 9, for after-school programs in sports, fitness and culture. Under the measure, each year the state – its' finances permitting – gives up to $50,000 to elementary schools, up to $75,000 to junior highs, and additional grants of up to $200,000 for schools with students coming predominantly from low-income families."[17] Maybe Arnold should add an addendum to his motto mentioned above. Help those who need help in the same manner as those that helped you become successful.

Arnold has been elected the governor of California and it seems to have gotten rather exciting in Sacramento. The state presently has budget problems which have caused some great one liners to hit the evening news on a regular basis. Can you imagine what the state budget is going to look like if he doesn't get it passed through the way he wants it? The replacement glass and furniture for the capital building will be enormous. Just think, when one senator or representative adds some pork to one of his bills and Governor Arnold tells him to remove it and he doesn't. Scene 1 Take 1: Governor Arnold (GA) "Senator, let's go outside and talk about this impasse", then GA picks up the Senator and throws him through the window and casually strolls down the stairs while lighting up a Cohibas. Yes I know. He would not throw him/her out a window but I'm sure as hell not going to be the one to tell him he has to put out the cigar because of California's silly ass smoking laws. Then there is a movement to have him run for the US Senate. I will endorse him only if he promises to take the majority of

---

[17] Ibid: 73.

his weapons with him and clean house so we can start with a clean slate. This way would be cheaper than the proposed CCPP and not voting for an incumbent (just a thought). I feel your pain Mr. S. I married into a rather liberal family myself, but just in case you are still passing out those humidors that were mentioned in the article, I'll pay for the shipping.

Martha Stewart

CCP # 43,000. If you do not know who this is, welcome back, that must have been a hell of an accident you were in to induce such a long coma. What was this person thinking when she was dumping that stock; that no one would notice? If she was not the CEO of a multi-million dollar corporation, the blonde bimbo act might have worked, but that is doubtful since her previous job was as a registered stock broker. On June 4, 2003, a Federal Grand Jury in New York City indicted the "Porcelain Princess" (nothing sticks to her) on obstruction of justice, conspiracy, securities fraud and lying to investigators. With all of this the Security Exchange Commission is going after her in civil court as well. If she is found guilty and receives jail time, can we assume she will see a side of the world that will produce such an extreme form of "Cultural Shock" on the Princess as to force the prison management to place her on suicide watch? Let's face it, the color schemes in prison would surely send any "Decorating Diva" over the edge. And we all know that if the prison officials force her to wear a uniform that has those black and white horizontal strips on it. Lord knows, no fashion guru would be caught dead in horizontal strips, this would be grounds for appeal under the Constitutional amendment for cruel and unusual punishment.

Martha placed a full page ad in USA Today on June 5, 2003, telling her fans and supporters of her innocence. The big bad government is coming after poor little Martha because she is a successful businesswoman in a man's world. I have a hard time believing this because the founder of ImClone Systems, Samuel Waksal, has pled guilty to the charges against him and he is willing to take his punishment. But then again, maybe Martha and her attorney are right. The government is really trying to railroad the "Queen of Décor" to one of their establishments. We all know the government is going through budget crunches. What better way for the Federal Department of Corrections to save money on remodeling than by having an inmate with these types of credentials, instead of paying a huge sum of money to consultants. Think about it; everyone of us would get despondent going to work where everything is painted in that government gray. The first thing Martha will do is get rid of the GI issued sheets and just think what the meals in the cafeteria are going to start looking like. Who knows, maybe this could become a source of income for the Department of Corrections by allowing the public to eat at the facility on weekends. But the down side to this scenario is to look at how many Martha Stewart clones the world will have to endure when all of these women are released from prison, because you know with her personality, Martha is going to teach everyone her way of life so the world will look prettier.

The upside to this is that Martha will have time to watch some of her competitors on TV. Shows such as TLC's "Trading Spaces" and "While You Were Out" could be part of her rehabilitation and education, and shows like "This Old House," "House Beautiful," and "Home Again" could be seen as electives. This would be expanding Martha's creative horizons, and for a graduate degree she could watch the Christopher Lowell show on the Discovery Channel, since the world knows the most creative interior designers are gay men. Who knows, after a few years behind bars, Martha's changes to the cells may be shown in magazines such as "Home and Garden,"

"Southern Living," or could spawn a new journal such as "Cell Beautiful."

Ex-President Bill Clinton

CCP # 68 (you do me and I owe you one). All of America knows he is not taking this retirement gig easy. We feel his pain. He left a job where he was on call 24/7 and now he is experiencing withdrawal pains in the same manner as a drug addict. Power is addictive and when you no longer have it, you can experience an empty feeling. At one time in his life, in his bag he had all the tools he needed to show the world he had the power. Tools such as B1 bombers, cruise missiles, aircraft carriers, along with all of the other hardware that the military has to play with; this is truly the definition of powerful. Today, all he has is a 3 wood and the decision to go for the green in 2, over water of course, or take a 7 iron and lay up. You can play golf only so many days a week and speaking from experience, no one controls that game, not even a man that was once known as "The most powerful man in the free world." Bill's wife, Hillary, just did an interview with Barbara Walters on Sunday, June 8, 2003, launching her book tour. During the interview, Hillary tells the story of Bill telling her the truth regarding Monica. What Hillary does not tell the American public is the rest of the story. Every man in America who has been caught cheating on his wife and knows he has to tell her the truth would want to have the same situation that Bill had. What was that you wonder? Two armed Secret Services agents were standing directly behind him with guns drawn. Rumor has it the female agent offered Hillary her weapon.

Lately, President Clinton has been making inquires into changing the US Constitution regarding the number of times a person can be president. Bill, get over it. There maybe a Clinton in the White House in the future, but it won't be you.

So the little woman is now the bread winner of the family. Your platform said women should be paid the same as men. But I must admit, I would not be to happy being known as "The First Kept Man" if my wife was elected president. Look at the bright side - if she is elected, he will get to be one of those government people who will be double dipping. He will get his retirement and then he will get the expense money that is usually allocated to the First Lady. And with that extra money he might be able to afford the green fees at Pebble Beach.

Dick Clark

CCP # ONLY GOD KNOWS, this man/creature/alien has been around so long, while never aging a day. Rumor has it that when the first caveman created the flute, Dick was there to rate it. I think most of the CCPs have seen Dick's autobiography that was made into a movie, "Highlander." You know, the one where the hero lives forever, unless he gets his head cut off. You doubt this because he is not the big strapping man that is in the movie. It was the unauthorized biography of Clark so they took artistic liberties. Dick is truly an alien because if he is human, he has the best plastic surgeon on retainer. If the latter is true, please give Michael Jackson this person's name and telephone number.

I know several preachers down south that claim this man was one of the main reasons the country is in the state it is in today. Rock and Roll was devil-sent and here was this man pumping out sin to the youth of our country without any shame. He is truly the Anti-Christ. I didn't think about that. He wouldn't age either, would he? All of that bumping and grinding on his show led to the sexual revolution. I do not know if that is true or not, but if it is, then I, for one, am here to thank you. Lord knows we had some fun times in my younger years.

The man is very open minded because he kept bringing us every new form of music that came out of the production studios and trust me some of it was down right crappy. His shows ranged from Do Wop, Rock & Roll, War protest songs, Heavy Metal, Disco, Big Hair Bands, and Hip Hop so take your pick. Some of these periods were not mankind's finest hour. If your mother's prediction of you going deaf for listening to that music so loud is true, why is Dick still around? Is he totally deaf and he is just a lip reading machine? Or is he truly one of the aliens that crashed at Roswell and his hearing is capable of handling up to 500 DBs? It keeps coming back to that alien thing, doesn't it?

Hugh Hefner

CCP # 00, (I could not get the computer to put two little dots in the center of the two zeros) this man is the envy of every male CCP in the world. Hugh has seen more boobs in his lifetime than the New Orleans Superdome filled with a convention of OB/GYN's. Hugh gives a whole new meaning to that old saying "Lucky Stiff." This younger generation grew up with the saying "I want to be just like Mike" (that is Michael Jordan for all you old farts); not my generation of males. We wanted to be just like Hugh. Hell, if we couldn't be Hugh, we just wanted to be one of his "Quality Control Inspectors" thus insuring Hugh only got the best. This man truly did help bring on the "Sexual Revolution." Maybe if we start a petition we can get the ball rolling for the Pope to appoint him as a Saint. Saint Hugh of the Silicon Boobs… Kinda has a ring to it, don't you think?

Do you remember years ago when Playboy made a major change in the magazine? That change was to take the staple out of the navel of the centerfold. See, Hugh was a man that could foresee the future with all of the body piercing. Today, the staple can go back into the navel and no one will think anything about it. Look at what this man did for the literacy of this country. Every time a man was seen buying the magazine, the first words out of his mouth were, "I don't look at the pictures, I buy it for the articles", and that was just the preachers and politicians. Hugh should have a Honorary Doctorate degree in education. Look at how many young boys he taught art, fashion, transportation, sex education, and of course, female anatomy. I recently saw an interview with Saint Hugh. In the program he stated the greatest medical breakthrough in the 20th Century was that little blue pill, Viagra. Can I get an Amen, brother! In that same program it showed the Saint out partying and dancing with five top-heavy blondes and at the end of the program it shows the night ending with everyone heading into his bedroom. Now that was truly a fairly tale because for that man, at his age, to have been able to take care of all of those women he would have had to have taken so much Viagra that he would have developed a permanent "Woody." When he dies, the undertaker will have to take a crowbar to his "Johnson" in order to get the lid shut. But then again, his magazine always did have some good fantasy in it.

Andrew Luster

CCP # TBA (the California Department of Correction will be issuing this number) For all of you CCPs that do not watch the news and do not have a clue who this guy is, let me describe him as the **DUMBEST** white boy God ever pumped breath into. I refuse to call him a man for the sick things he did to women. Why do I feel this way about this low life? Simple. The things he did to the women that were not necessary. This guy did not have the Hollywood looks that were going to get his picture on GQ or any other magazine, he does not have the looks that will put him in movies, but he did have something that would make women flock to him, MONEY. This stupid bastard was the heir to a fortune from the Max Factor make-up empire and it was not likely that he would ever go broke. Even in a bad economy, make-up is going to be purchased on a regular basis. What was the crime this snake was found guilty of? If we listed all the charges, this chapter would be approximately an additional 100 pages. Putting the "Date Rape" drug in women's drinks and then taking them to his home. Once at his house, he would video tape the act of raping them. Note to Andrew: In prison, you will not be lucky enough to be passed out when Bubba is raping you. Did you ever hear that old saying "Whatever goes around comes around?" Didn't this idiot listen to his mommy and daddy when they were teaching him that life lesson that states, "Money can buy anything?" All he had to do was get the latest copy of the "Gold Diggers Hall of Fame" roster and he would have been able to find a woman that would have done any of the sick acts that he wanted to participate in and, guess what, he would not have gone to prison. Andrew, remember that other saying that you hear around Christmas time, "It is better to give than to receive." You are about to meet a group of men that truly believe in that saying and will be giving it to you for the next 124 years.

Michael Jackson

CCP # 5 (just think there a four brothers and some sisters), this family proves those old statements are true and the family portrait could be found on two posters proclaiming these statements. 1. Money can't buy happiness and 2. We put the **fun** in the word dysfunctional. The man is truly a musical genius but we all know how fine the line that separates genius and insanity is, don't we? How many times do you reckon Michael has driven his go-cart from one side of the line to the other? We have all watched Michael grow up, at least in stature, from a little boy to his teen years, although puberty is still in question. We were there when he became a young man and we all have observed his latest transformation into something else. The alien chapter responded to my request to research their files and to no avail, this creature is a new life form that even they have never encountered. I know students have received Doctorate degrees from universities regarding the Metamorphosis of larva into butterflies and other creatures in nature go through changes in their life time, but Michael is truly baffling the scientific community. They do not know if it is the environment in his home, a ranch called "Never Land." Did he purposely leave out one word. Should it read "Never Never Land," or have these changes been brought on through genetic mutation? What if all of the "EMP" (electronic magnetic pulse) emitted from all of the lights and speakers from the shows, the sound waves from the speakers, along with the Pepsi flowing in his body, and then his head catching fire (the fire is obviously the catalyst) the change started taking place? It could happen. When he came out of the hospital he became very reclusive didn't he? What other CCPs do you know that are in their right mind (I know I am asking a lot here, but go with the flow) that went out in public wearing one glove and later a mask. Who knows? Maybe he is just starting to deflate and is caving in on himself starting with his nose. But again, things such as this metamorphosis and all the other studies that end in "osis" are above my pay grade to comprehend, so I will just watch with millions of other CCPs to see what comes out next. Damn, I forgot about the possibility of Evolution, but then again that is another whole thesis.

8. TELEVISION AND HOW IT HAS AFFECTED OUR LIVES

"You see these preachers on TV in a suit and a tie and vest. They want you to give your money to the Lord, but they give you their address." ... Hank Williams, Jr.

Today in our great society, there are two camps of CCPs and each is just as devout in their beliefs as the other. These beliefs deal with the theories of the world's creation. The "Creationists" believe that God created the world in seven days; the "Evolutionists" believe in Darwin's Theory of Evolution. The creationists do not believe that evolution exists in any form or manner, and the evolutionists say science proves they are correct. But, they are missing one important fact, the elusive "Missing Link." Well, maybe I can help enlighten the creationist and show that evolution does take place in modern man, or maybe I have found the "Missing Link," thus proving the Darwin theory. You think this will make me eligible for a Nobel Prize? Just follow along with my theory and see if it justifies my claim.

The Greatest Invention of Mankind

I can hear all of you now expressing your own opinion as to what this invention is. I am here to tell you, one and all, it is the ***TELEVISION REMOTE CONTROL!*** There is no doubt about it! This one instrument has brought about more changes in the way man watches TV more than another historical piece of technology. Of course it has brought about divorces, business failures, and fights in sports bars as well. But all inventions have a few negative effects and there's always a downside till the bugs are worked out. Let's face it. Cars and airplanes have crashes and this negativity does not cause a decline in sales. Here's a little history in the evolution of TV watching:

In the 1950s, man had three networks to watch: ABC, CBS and NBC. When a man wanted to see what was on, he had to get out of his command module, a.k.a. recliner for you CCPs with short memories, walk across the room, and flip through the channels. Of course, no self-respecting male CCP would look in the TV Guide to see what was playing. The scenario just described would only take place in a single male CCP's home, because if he had kids, he would have screamed at one of them to come into the room and turn the channel. And, if was he stupid enough to scream at his wife, telling her to come in and change the channel, she would have told him to do something to himself that is physically impossible to do. This scenario would continue for another twenty years.

The 1960s brought color TV to the masses of CCPs. How many times did we hear this cute little jingle: "The following show is being brought to you in living color." Man had thought he had reached Nirvana, but then again, you have to remember that mans' way of thinking back then was just a step out of the Stone Age. So what if we have gone to the moon and back? We are talking about the mainstay of the family, TELEVISION! Only the rich and famous were the lucky ones that had remote controls in their households. Some ingenious CCPs (usually single) would pay a neighborhood kid to come into his house to change the channels for him so he would not have to leave the command module. You have to remember that with the onset of cable, man had more than three channels to watch. I'm not claiming these channels were worth a damn, but there were more channels to look at. And with the Beach Boys playing on the radio, a new term in CCP language was invented, CHANNEL SURFING.

The 1970s brought the "Holy Grail" to the masses. The remote was the rage of the 70's in the same manner that color TV was for the 60's. As with all the rules regarding the laws of the jungle and only the strongest being able to survive, the remote became a tool of the man in the household. The remote holds a special place in a man's heart. Only his "Johnson" takes precedent over the remote. Take a close look at the facts. This is the one and only thing a man could control in his household. Does anyone believe that silly old saying "A man's home is his castle?" This was obviously said by a woman, thus giving man a false sense of security.

The 1980s were mind boggling for all of the CCPs with so many channels and not enough time in the day to watch them. Then there was that one little problem that kept getting in the way of man truly reaching Television Nirvana, work. He still had to go to work to pay the cable bill, and to ensure he did his job properly, he had to sleep, which in turn cut into his TV time. But now the channels had some substance to them. There were 24-hour news channels such as CNN, as well as The Weather Channel and, of course, The Playboy Channel. Now, being the world traveled sophisticated man that I am, I did not pay extra on my cable bill to receive the Playboy channel when I received the National Geographic channel for free. Most men will not admit this true statement, but it is passed down from father to son since the beginning of time. You can look at Playboy or National Geographic and you are looking at sights you are never going to visit so why waste your money. So, since it was free, I watched the National Geographic channel as often as possible. Oh, did I mention, ESPN became a serious sports channel during this time. And most important, along with the cablevision box came that coveted, cherished, and worshipped instrument, "The REMOTE."

With the onset of the 1990s, another level of man's evolution was reached. Satellite television was introduced in a manner that every household could have one and it did not require an acre of land to be installed on. With this new tool (this rates right up there with fire, the wheel, heart transplants, etc.), man had even more channels to watch along with some foreign channels, thus expanding our every evolving mind. And, of course, along with this new piece of equipment in the house came a newer bigger remote. You have to love this country.

The new millennium did not introduce any new remote controls, but it did issue in new television products such as HDTV, TiVo, and plasma screens. All of these new tools will be discussed later on in the chapter.

As stated earlier in this thesis, the remote was the only object in the house the man was in control of. Women had a hard time adjusting to this new age of evolution. Losing control was not easy for them. For years, women controlled men with the promise of sex. Men would clean the yard and pick up after themselves in hopes of reaching the promised land occasionally. After years of broken dreams, men were elated to finally have something that they controlled in the house. So what did the coalition of women come up with to negate this control? Hide the remote. What did this accomplish? Everything that they wanted, because the remote only worked with the TV it came with. And then came the second greatest invention of man and this was brought on to counteract the women's coalition movement, **THE UNIVERSAL REMOTE**. The man that invented this piece of equipment should be ranked up there with Thomas Edison and Albert Einstein.

I know my thesis was short regarding the evolution of man and television, but it has merit. Man has evolved from the Stone Age of the 50s to the Space Age of the 90s, so this proves that Darwin was right, because the missing link is the typical American male CCP.

Programming and Enlightenment

In these modern times, you can find a channel for just about every subject known to mankind. You have the sewing network, the golf channel, C-SPAN, hunting with Bubba, fishing with Cooter. Then you have educational channels such as Discovery, TLC (The Learning Channel), amongst a host of others and then there is one that is dedicated to showing different surgical operations. I never caught the name of that channel but I must admit it was very interesting.

One night while channel surfing, a favorite past time of mine, I happened to catch this channel. It was showing an operation that would make every straight male CCP break down in tears… it was a breast reduction operation. It should be against the law that this type of operation is performed in the Good Ol' US of A. Every male, straight men, of course, from the time he sees his first Playboy, dreams of climbing to (maybe I should have used the word "on" here) those heights. Every woman I know with big breasts has made the same statement, "They are too heavy and they hurt my back." Well that is what you get for being so selfish and carrying them bad boys around by yourself. As I have mentioned to these women on several occasions, every straight male CCP in the country is willing to help share the load. If every big breasted woman in America walked into a room full of men and said at the top of her lungs "My boobs are killing my back, will someone hold them up for me?" she would have to leave the room because of the riot she just created due to all of the men trying to be the first in line to help her. See, that shoots down the theory that the male CCPs are not willing to share and get in touch with the (my wife just informed me that the correct word here is "their" but my version sounds better and would be truly more effective) feminine side.

Another surgery that I watched was an arthroscopy knee operation. This was very near and dear to my heart since I was going to have my third one in a few weeks. My previous Orthopedic surgeon was back in Florida. This gentleman had done the two previous knee operations and a AC shoulder operation (did I mention before that I used to play football) and I had great faith and trust in this man. But, now I lived in Washington and my insurance would not pay if I went to Florida to have this work done there. My new surgeon came highly recommended, so the date was set for June 28, 1996. At this particular hospital, to help prevent accidents, the patient, along with a spouse/family member, is sent to a nice relaxing waiting area to meet with the anesthesiologist to discuss the different procedures, and then the Doctor comes in to explain his portion of the procedure. When the anesthesiologist asked about my previous operations and asked what I wanted, I replied "a spinal". He asked me why and I said I did not know this doctor and I wanted to see if he doing the job right.

In the Operating Room, the anesthesiologist gives me the shot and I cannot feel anything from my chest down. The doctor is to my left, which is really good since it's the left knee he is suppose to work on, and to my right there is a large TV monitor for the doctor to watch while he is inside my knee. I already feel safe knowing the doctor is a CCP, since he's got a TV right there. Directly in front of me, they have placed a curtain blocking my view, and after the third time straining my neck to see the doctor and the monitor, the doctor asks me if I wanted to watch to which I reply "Hell Yes!" After they removed the curtain and I was lying there watching the monitor, the program I watched on the Discovery Channel the previous evening came to mind. Earthquakes in the Northwest and how they were expecting Seattle to experience a quake that registers 9 or better on the Richter scale. And where was I? Lying paralyzed from the chest down, in DOWNTOWN SEATTLE! I looked down at the foot of the operating table and saw a very large male nurse and asked him if he would mind standing by the head of the table (the doctor told me ahead of time this nurse was in the room to observe only). The nurse complied with my request but asked me why I wanted him at the head of the table, so I related the above-mentioned TV story and my fears of not being able to leave the room if a quake hit. The nurse smiled and said "What makes you think I would take you with me?" And I replied that I was sure he would want his balls with him and I would guarantee him if a quake hit my right hand would clamp on them like a vice. When the doctors and nurses quit laughing, well except for the male nurse, the operation resumed. Remember the meeting with the doctor prior to the operation? He informed my wife and myself that the entire operation would be recorded on video and a copy would go home with us. It was right after the laughter died down the anesthesiologist did something and then out loud said "Oops!" The doctor looked at him and said that was not very smart thing to do and he (gas passer) asked why. The doctor pointed at me and said, "His wife is a lawyer." The next thing the anesthesiologist said was "Oh Shit!" and the second thing he said "Is the audio on?" I laughed and said "I am willing to bet even odds that it is on but on my copy it will just be video." When I got home and watched the tape, the images were outstanding. All that was missing was the piano player because it was definitely a silent movie.

Three Years Later

I am watching the "Surgery Channel" again but this time it deals with a prostate operation. To this day my GP doctor wants to know why it is so tough to give me the exam. After watching that, can we say pucker factor comes into play here? And, of course, the next day I am back at the same hospital in Seattle about to have my left knee worked on again. My wife and I are back in that nice relaxing waiting area along with several other patients and their family members. Once you have been admitted to the hospital, the patient is given a wristband that has all of his/her pertinent information on it. This wristband is checked every time someone from the hospital comes up to talk with you or exams you. Hell, they even check your wristband when you come out of the bathroom to ensure you are the same person that went in there. My wife and I had been waiting in the room long enough to read all of the Reader's Digests and Modern Living magazines when the receptionist walks up to us and says, "The delay is due to complications in the operating room that was scheduled for you." First of all, the word "complications" is not a word I want to hear from anyone, especially someone that works in the hospital. Jeannie and I look around and, sure enough, she and I are the only people left in the room. Then the lady tells us the anesthesiologist will be down shortly to speak with me.

About ten minutes later, a gentleman wearing surgical clothing arrives with a folder in hand, grabs my wrist, checks the band against the folder's title and sits down. The first thing he said was, "I see that you are recently married. Congratulations." Now, Jeannie and I had been married for over six years and if he considered that recent, who am I to argue? The next question came out of left field. No it came out of the parking lot about a mile past left field. "When you finally can achieve an erection, does it lean to the right or the left?" After I got up off the floor,

I told him I hoped he was referring to my political preference, because the last time I looked, my "Johnson" pointed straight and did not have any problems coming (get your mind out of the gutter) to attention. I then informed him that I was there to have my **LEFT KNEE** operated on, not my "Weenie." The man then he explained he was an Urologist. I told him the doctor I was expecting had a vowel at the beginning of his specialty but it started with an **O**. And being married to a smart ass as well, Jeannie could not pass up the opportunity to pass him one of her business cards. I thought we were going to have to perform CPR on the man from the look on his face. He ran to the receptionist's desk, screaming at her for giving him the wrong folder and pointing out the wrong patient. The only problem was that when he came in, the receptionist was in the bathroom, and he picked up the wrong folder and there was no one in the room except Jeannie and myself. When the correct doctor arrived we told him what had just happened. I got worried that he would not be able to operate on me because he was laughing so hard he was crying. I was afraid that he might start laughing during the operation and that would not be good. He told Jeannie and myself that he knew this doctor and he was going to inform some of the other doctors, so the Urologists could never live it down. Footnote: Two years later I was back to have the same knee operated on again. Only, this time I was taking some extra precautions. Written on the right knee was **NO** and taped to it was my wife's business card, and I was wearing a cup.

So if you have learned anything from my experiences with the medical community, I hope that it's "Don't watch any television prior to going into the hospital." You especially do not want to watch any medical dramas and if you happen to come across the Surgery Channel, remove that channel from the programming in your remote. Just remember that old saying "Ignorance is bliss."

New Fangled Televisions

Every male CCP knows that the television he wants in his castle goes against everything Martha Stewart stands for. But, just hang in there for a little while because Martha may be out of the picture for quite a few years and if you know your history, after any dictator is dethroned, there is a power vacuum with all of the underlings vying for the top spot, and in this short period of time fashion/design anarchists will run amuck. There are televisions out there now that would send Tim Allen's character, Tim Taylor in Home Improvement, into grunting ecstasy. There are televisions that fit in your hand and we are not talking about a picture so bad that you will need glasses after watching five minutes. NO, we are talking HDTV quality. There are screens that will cover one entire wall, and least we not forget PLASMA TV. This is the real reason that Home Improvement was discontinued. Tim Taylor attended one of the electronic conferences in Las Vegas and all of the stimulation he got in the TV section of the room was more that his sensory inputs could handle. When the EMTs arrived, at first they were confused. They did not know if Tim was having a sexual experience or an out of body experience. One thing that I know for sure, Tim's a lucky man because when they put the paddles on him, as they do on most heart attack victims, his body discharged more electricity that the machine could handle (Tim has worked out a monthly arrangement to pay for the machine), thus burning up the unit along with the carpet he was laying on. There may not be spontaneous human combustion in the world, but you have just read proof of male Sensory Electronic Overload (SEO). So ladies and significant others, to ensure the male of your house survives SEO, follow these two simple rules: 1) Do not allow him to attend any electronic show/conference. 2) If you cannot keep him away from the show, attach a ground wire to him and allow it to drag on the carpet thus discharging any charge build up. Oh, and do not touch him or any other male that is attending the show because the electrical discharge could be hazardous to your hairstyle. Of course, adding ground wires to these men would also bring about changes in the local/national fire and electrical codes.

Nowadays there are TVs that will record the show you are watching and play back part of it or all of it in the same manner as instant replay. If they ever develop a TV that allows you to hit a button that will skip the commercial, that will rate up there as when man walked on the moon. What can I say, even Einstein could only think so far into the future.

And let's not stop here with the Television. Think of all of the other attachments that you can add to your TV to make it become the "Ultimate Entertainment Center" of the neighborhood. There is Surround Sound. This has become so realistic that your front door has to have a warning on it telling guests that your house is equipped with this equipment. Just think of the consequences if you invite an uninformed guest (especially if they are from California) and you turn on the movie "Earthquake." You will have to perform CPR or the neighbors will wonder why people came running and screaming out of your home.

The VCR for years was the third greatest invention of mankind (remember remote and universal remote are 1 & 2). You could watch any movie without commercial interruption. This feature played hell on your bladder until your kids showed you the pause button. What true male CCP ever read the directions first? Furthermore, why do they put those damn papers in the box anyway? And then you found that rewind button. That day rates right up there with your first beer, your first home run, your first car, the day you got married (Ok, so it doesn't rate up there with your wedding date, but it is as important as that date, isn't it?). Then the kids taught you how to program the VCR to record, and your world was complete. You truly could die a happy man. Women have known for years it does not take much to amuse men. And the female CCPs are not immune from the record button ecstasy. How many episodes of soap operas along with QVC and the Home Shopping Network have ended up on miles of magnetic tape?

DVDs. What more can be said about these fantastic machines? The pictures on this equipment are so real I caught myself watching a Bruce Willis movie the other night from behind my recliner because I was using it for protection. Bruce had so much lead flying around the room I was afraid of getting hit by a stray bullet. Even DD (my dog) ran out of the room to go help Lassie find Timmy on one show. Have you heard the latest regarding courtroom drama? The movie studios are suing a software company that will allow you to copy your own DVDs. Doesn't this remind you of the lawsuit that Disney, Sony and other movie makers brought to court in the early 80s because VCRs were going to take away their profits? Guess what, the movie industry's profits increased. They had profit margins that were higher than they could have ever dreamed of and most of the time video sales are larger that the box office sales. How many films have become "Cult Classics" due to video sales that were bombs at the box office? Once again the big industry is afraid it might miss collecting a single penny. All CCPs know that the Hollywood movie companies are the most honest, forthright industry in the nation, and they want to ensure that the writers and actors are protected and get what is due to them. And if you believe that, you are the most gullible person on this planet (after a poll of the alien chapter was taken, none of its members believe that line, so that would put you out in the galaxy by yourself). They are not bringing on this legal action for themselves, they are happy with what small percentage of a film they get. Give me a break.

Now you can get DVDs for your car to entertain the little darlings on a long trip, such as to the local McDonalds. Lord knows we do not want to interact with said darlings as if carrying on a conversation was outlawed, or let them read a book. How archaic am I? I am willing to allow the book to have pictures in it since the majority of the kids are "reading challenged." A PC police officer was looking over my shoulder while writing that sentence. She seemed happy that I am coming along nicely in my journey to find my inner self. The entertainment centers in some of these cars are more expensive that the model of car that most CCPs drive. I am not against technology, but let's face it, we have enough problems on the road with people just trying to drive in an orderly manner. You have to remember a good number of these people are eating, reading, talking on a cell phone, applying make-up, sleeping, along with a host of other activities, while trying to drive and now we are going to let them watch a movie. What next: the center console turns into a popcorn maker?

Speaking of cell phones, what in God's green earth is this world coming to? Again the standard answer "Hell in a hand basket." The every day annoying cell phone has become a mini-computer/phone/fax/camera/game center along with a host of other operations. Now instead of hearing someone screaming to a person across country while you are trying to eat in the restaurant, you now get to hear the following sounds, receiving a fax, connecting to the internet, "You've got mail!" "Hold that pose while I take your picture," and last but not least, some video hero blasting the hell out of a three headed monster, and all of this takes place before you get your salad.

How many of you remember the old TV cartoon, "The Jetsons?" And how many times have you heard the female gender of the CCPs state, "There is no way I am ever going to have a video phone?" And why did they make that statement? Pure and simple VANITY, that's why. Do you really think that they would allow someone to see them without their make up properly painted on and have this picture transmitted through the air waves via video phone when they will not even go to the mail box without a day of beauty from their favorite spa? And who is buying these new camera phones? WOMEN! Why are they buying these phones that they swore would never be in their household? Because they are catty, conniving bitches, that's why. This new technology brings the gossip mill up to a higher plane. Ladies, how many times have you been in a store and seen your biggest rival in an outfit you would not be seen wearing at a Luau, or the colors are so bright and gaudy that they would make a seeing eye dog change directions? In the old days you would have to go home and call your inner circle of friends and describe what you saw. Recently you could call said friends on your cell phone and give them a play-by-play blow of the fashion blunder. Nowadays you can take a picture of the Diva Gone Bad, post it on the world wide web (why share it with your limited number of friends - let the world experience this fashion suicide), as well as e-mailing this to Mr. Black as a nominee for his worst dressed list. Men, what is the worst thing that can happen to you? Someone catches you picking your nose or scratching your ass. Who cares because we all know that fashion statements in public is not one of our high priorities. If a person invents a phone where a man can dial a number and hold the phone over a mug and out comes his favorite beer, dials another number and two tickets to a sporting event is printed out, and another number for sex, then that person will make Bill Gates look like a homeless person. Let's all face it, men have their priorities and fashion ain't on the list.

Flat Screen And Plasma Television

Progress and Evolution are both wonderful things. CCPs have gone from the Stone Age black & white televisions to the

Iron Age. This would be the introduction of color. Progress continued through the Industrial Age which would be the period the remote was delivered to the masses and finally we are in the Space Age with man having the ability to watch television in bed lying flat on his back. The reason people no longer have to worry about getting neck strains from watching TV while lying down is due to that wonderful invention called the flat screen, which can be mounted on the ceiling. Living on the "Left Coast" which is also called the "Rim of Fire" due to all of the volcano activity, which in turns causes earthquakes, I will not install a TV over my head, even though my ex-wives claim my head is as hard as concrete. With the introduction of flat screen and plasma, explosions are grander, watching a car wreck in a Nascar race gives you the feeling you are in the passenger seat (that is, if they had one), you get the same sensations that a blitzing linebacker feels when he is about to blind side a quarterback, and last but not least, it takes T & A to a whole new level. If you have to ask what T&A is you will not be allowed to own one of these spectacular inventions.

I do not know what the future of television is going to evolve to in the next generation, and it is kind of scary to think that far ahead. Who knows what will literally come out of your TV. Remember the movie Poltergeist? That would definitely ruin your day if something reached from the TV and pulled you in. Then again it may depend on where it takes you, the place the little girl in Poltergeist went to? **NO.** Mary Ann's island of pain? **MAYBE.** The Playboy Channel? **THANK YOU LORD.** As I stated earlier, I don't know where we are going from here, but I do know where we have been, so stay tuned to see what happens next.

9.   IRAQ WAR

"The object of war is not to die for your country
but to make the other bastard die for his." . . . .
General George Patton

Deja Vu All Over Again

Some of you CCPs may want to skip this chapter since it will not be that funny and can be quite disturbing. We are lead down a path of doom and gloom by the elected officials that are supposed to be reporting the truth. If you don't want to read my ranting and raving in such a manner that it could piss off Rev. Billy Graham, my feelings won't be hurt if you skip ahead.

I will be the first to admit that I did not want to see our young people go to war in Iraq. When President Bush, Sr. would not let General Norman Schwartzkopf finish the job he started, we were bound to face "The Great Moronic Leader" again. When President Bush, Sr. let the Arab nations and the useless United Nations direct our policy, what was he thinking? This age of "Political Correctness" is going too far. When it's our men and women dying on a battlefield, who gives a rat's ass about what the U.N. thinks should be a fair peace treaty?

Let's take a close look at this impressive organization; it kind of favors a particular scene in The Wizard of Oz, with all of the smoke and loud rhetoric that comes out of it. Remember when Toto pulls the curtain back and revealed the "Great Powerful Wizard"? That is basically what we are seeing with the U.N. I have stated previously in this book that I can produce a number of people that will testify under oath that I am dumb, stupid and/or otherwise an ignorant Neanderthal, but I am going to show you insight into an organization that, if I was ever forced to work there, I would be regarded as a rocket scientist just due to what little common sense I have. In 2003, the U.N. made Libya head of the committee on Human Rights and Iraq head of the committee of Global Disarmament. What were these clowns thinking when they made these two countries head of anything? That would be like making Dr. Hannibal Lector the social director for a nudist colony. This is the same organization that paints all of its military equipment white and paints "U.N" in big blue letters on the side. The only place on earth this equipment could hide would be in an uprising in Siberia in the dead of winter. Why don't they just paint a bull's-eye on the equipment with a sign saying, "Shoot here!" The equipment I am talking about is for transportation only, God forbid, we give the soldiers guns to defend themselves. The U.N. is trying to look out for the soldiers. They have supplied them with vehicles that have four forward gears and sixteen gears in reverse. The U.N.'s new motto: "We do not know where we are going but we do know where we have been." Remember your ancient history lessons where the king of a country had a harem and the women were guarded by a group of men that had been castrated and those men were called eunuchs. Well, we have proof that just by cutting their testicles off did not stop some of these men from breeding, because their descendants can be found in New York City in the United Nations building. Never in the history of the world has such a large group of no-balls bastards assembled at one location. These guys and girls want to talk and have meetings while people are dying all over the world and heaven help us least they make a stand for anything.

Put yourself in Saddam's shoes after the Gulf War. How scared are you going to be when the U.N. inspectors pull up to the gate and ask permission to come in? Now which group do you think would have been more effective as inspectors, the U.N. eunuchs or the Army's 3rd infantry that uses an M-1 tank to roll through the gate and kicks the door down, ransacks the place, and then determines it is secure? On March 27, 2003, Hans Blix, the chief U.N. eunuch weapons inspector, made the statement that no treaty violation weapons have been found. The treaty said Iraq could not have SCUD missiles with a range of over 150 kms, but our troops in Kuwait have had to shoot down several SCUDs and they are over 190 kms away from the launching point. Then he made another stupid statement when a reporter informed him that there were missiles fired at Kuwait at distances greater than 150 km, and in response, the chief eunuch said, "Well, it was only a couple of kilometers further." Well, excuse the hell out of me; that is clearly a treaty violation. Hans, old boy, that is in the same league as if your mistress told you she could not get pregnant and yesterday she said she was four months late; ask your wife if that is a treaty violation. We have women in our military that have more balls that this inspector. The Iraqis don't have a chance. Let's face it men, how many years have we known how dangerous it is trying to argue with a woman with PMS? Now we're giving them M-16s and hand grenades. Dudes, prepare to meet Allah.

Trying To Help by Dennis Miller

All the rhetoric on whether or not we should go to war against Iraq has got my insane little brain spinning like a roulette wheel. I enjoy reading opinions from both sides but I have detected a hint of confusion from some of you. As I was reading the paper recently, I was reminded of the best advice someone ever gave me. He told me about the KISS method. This means "Keep It Simple, Stupid!" So, with this as a theme, I'd like to apply this theory for those who don't quite get it. My hope is that we can simplify things a bit and recognize a few important facts. Here are ten things to consider when voicing an opinion on this important issue:

1. Out of President Bush and Saddam Hussein . . . Hussein is the bad guy.

2. If you have faith in the United Nations to do the right thing, keep this in mind, they have Libya heading the Committee on Human Rights and Iraq heading the Global Disarmament Committee. Do your own math here.

3. If you use Google search and type in "French Military Victories," your reply will be "Did you mean French Military defeats?"

4. If your only Anti-war slogan is "No War For Oil," sue your school district for allowing you to slip through the cracks and robbing you of the education you deserve.

5. Saddam and Bin Laden will not seek United Nations approval before they try to kill us.

6. Despite common belief, Martin Sheen is not the President. He plays one on TV.

7. Even if you are anti-war, you are still an "Infidel!" and Bin Laden wants you dead, too.

8. If you believe in a "vast right-wing conspiracy" but not in the danger that Hussein poses, quit hanging out with the Dell computer dude.
9. We are going to liberate them.
10. Whether you are for military action or against it, our young men and women overseas are fighting for us to defend our right to speak out. We all need to support them without reservation.

There is no doubt about it Dennis Miller is definitely a CCP.

Opinions

Everyone has the right to voice their opinion and that is the great thing about this country. A good amount of men and women died for all of us to have that right and when anyone takes that right for granted, it pisses me off. With that said, I agree with the little old lady in this next story. A lady was commuting to Washington D.C. on the subway due to the anti-war protests on the major roads leading into the city. It was raining, so everyone knows this just adds to the confusion of traveling. When she entered the subway station, a young, twenty-something female tried to hand her an anti-war flyer and she refused, then the young female tried to hand the flyer to an elderly woman and that woman refused as well. The young female then touched the elderly woman on the shoulder and said "Don't you want to know about the children dying in Iraq?" The elderly lady turned around and said "Honey, my first husband died in France during World War II so that you would have the right to protest, but if you ever touch me again, I will shove this umbrella up your ass and open it." AMEN! Why was that young female not out there protesting when Saddam was gassing all of the cities that were opposing him?

Have you noticed all of the coverage this war is getting? It's all over the television twenty-four hours a day, seven days a week. Never in the history of the human race has a war been so well documented. Every channel has gone out and hired any retired military personnel that they can find. The bigger the network, the higher-ranking officers. ABC, CBS, NBC, FOX and CNN all have Generals and Admirals on their staff. The local channels are able to find some Colonels and Navy Captains to help them, but when you get way down the list in the TV Guide, you take what you can get. You know what I mean. The Food Channel and VH-1. Word has it The Food Channel is holding a séance trying to bring back Colonel Sanders and VH-1 was attending the same meeting trying to get Elvis' old manager to help them. Remember Colonel Parker? That shows you the extremes these marketing people will go to in order to stay with the topic of the day.

Speaking of food, I want to know who the "Suck Ass" was, in either the Capital Building or The White House that took it upon his or herself to rename French fries and French toast to **"FREEDOM FRIES, FREEDOM TOAST."** The person that came up with this heart-stirring ideal has way too much time on their hands and is definitely being over paid. As my cousin Wewa always says, ten minutes of ass kissing is better than ten years of seniority. If that is true, then the person that came up with the new menu items should be able to suck a bowling ball through a fifty-foot garden hose. The sad news is that this person is more than likely a card-carrying CCP and has bred and brought little suck asses into the world and there is no way we can revoke his/ her card. This is definitely one for the rules committee.

Combat

I want to know why politicians who have never seen combat (and no, TV doesn't count), heard a bullet fly by them, or been so scared that they soiled their pants (having a reporter from the Washington Post outside your hotel room waiting for your mistress to come out does not count either) have the right to make the Rules of Engagements (ROE) for combat? Recently, the ROE stated that if an Iraqi soldier fired upon you, you could return fire. EXCUSE ME, aren't we at war? If you're an Iraqi soldier, or any other person, and have a weapon in your hand aiming at our countrymen and countrywomen, you should be exterminated with extreme prejudice. For all of you that did not understand the last sentence, it means your ticket to Allah has been purchased for you. To protect our young men and women, if you have a weapon, you just became a Target of Opportunity and I do not care what they use to help you on your way to paradise, be it a M-16, M-60, 50 cal., Smart Bomb or whatever. When you picked up a weapon, you just had a bull's-eye tattooed onto your forehead.

These same idiot politicians are trying to handcuff our military even more with these stupid ROE. I was watching the news when the announcer stated that U.S. forces had surrounded this town and was taking fire from the local militants, or whatever they are called this week, and these holy warriors were holed up in the local Mosque. We, the ever-loving "Politically Correct Good Guys" will not destroy the building and/or any other historic or cultural buildings. Now I understand why other countries do not like us. We are so sweet that we could put most diabetics in a coma. Have you ever noticed that most of our politicians were the geeks in school? They were the hall monitors or the homeroom teacher's pet, so now they're trying to do the same things on a larger scale. The ROE should read, "If you (insert "enemy" term here) go in a building, then it means it must not be important to your heritage or religion, and that means it is not important to us. Stick a weapon out of the window and fire at our troops. It just became real important to us, and the count down for your meeting with Allah just began." Trust me, it will not be long, because the Time Over Target is not long. That sound you hear is a Marine Corp issued F-18 Hornet with a smart bomb with your name all over it. The easiest way not to see a bomb up close and personal is to sit in the building and pray, unarmed of course, but if you do decide to stick the gun out the window, ask the organist if they know that old Roy Rogers' tune "Happy Trails."

All that the PC people and news media can say is "We are trying to win the hearts and mind of the Iraqi people." In winning the hearts and minds with all of these stupid ROE, they are endangering all of the coalition soldiers and sailors, but then again, these young people must be expendable. God forbid we endanger a gun-toting Iraqi. It seems our politicians forgot that when you've got them by the balls, their hearts and minds will follow.

On March 11, 2003, the U.S. Air Force tested the largest non-nuclear weapon in the history of the U.S. Up until this time the "Daisy Cutter" was the largest bomb in the arsenal weighing in at 14,500 pounds. The new bomb is called the MOAB, Massive Ordnance Air Blast (or, as the airmen and airwomen lovingly refer to it, the Mother Of All Bombs); this bad boy weighs in at 21,500 pounds. You will notice I called it a boy; we all know there is not a woman alive that is going to give her true weight. This weapon will not be used in a city, but in open areas on convoys, and such. This is a step in the right direction of winning the hearts and minds.

News Flash: Eglin Air Force Base, FL. – Air Force officials tested a Massive Ordnance Air Blast weapon here March 11, 2003. The MOAB is a precision-guided munition weighing 21,500 pounds and was dropped from a C-130 Hercules aircraft for the test. It is the largest non-nuclear weapon in existence. The aftershock was felt as far away as New Orleans, where shortly thereafter the French Quarter surrendered.

New U.S. Foreign Policy

1. The U.S. will apologize to the world for our "interference" in their affairs, past & present. You know, Hitler, Mussolini, Tojo and the rest of those "good old boys." We will never "interfere" again.

2. We will withdraw our troops from all over the world, starting with Germany, South Korea and the Philippines. They don't want us there. We would station troops at our borders. No more sneaking through holes in the fence.

3. All illegal aliens have 90 days to get their affairs together and leave. We'll give them a free trip home. After 90 days, the remainder will be gathered up and deported immediately, regardless of who or where they are. France would welcome them.

4. All future visitors will be thoroughly checked and limited to 90 days unless given a special permit. No one from a terrorist nation would be allowed in. If you don't like it there, change your government yourself; don't hide here. Asylum would not ever be available to anyone. We don't need any more cab drivers.

5. No "students" over the age of 21. The older ones are the bombers. If they don't attend classes, they get an "F" and it's back home baby.

6. The U.S. will make a strong effort to become self-sufficient energy wise. This will include developing non-polluting sources of energy, but will require a temporary drilling of oil in the Alaskan wilderness. The caribou will have to cope for a while.

7. Offer Saudi Arabia and other oil producing countries $10 a barrel for their oil. If they don't like it, we'll go someplace else.

8. If there is a famine or other natural catastrophe in the world, we will not "interfere." They can pray to their god for seeds, rain, cement or whatever they need. Besides, most of what we give them is stolen or given to the army. The people who need it most get very little, if any, anyway.

9. Ship the U.N. Headquarters to an island some place. We don't need the spies and fair weather friends here. Besides, it would make a good homeless shelter or lockup for illegal aliens.

10. All Americans must go to charm and beauty school. That way, no one can call us "Ugly Americans" any longer.

It seems the world hasn't liked America's attitude for the past sixty years, so lets see how they like this new one. I was not the author of the "New U.S. Foreign Policy." It was e-mailed to me, but it makes you stop and think. How many times has the U.S. arrived in a country to help them and, within days, we hear "Yankee Go Home!" Does this sound familiar? Two weeks after the Iraqi war is over, we hear that tune playing over and over again, so let's go home and let them fight amongst themselves to see who will govern the country.

I'm Back

It has been a couple of months since I have worked on this chapter because today's date is July 9, 2003. Since I last visited this site, Allied forces went through Iraq with such speed, it shocked all of the other countries that were following the campaign. The Russians were really upset since it was their military advisors that had trained Saddam's army, and the Germans were really upset because we had broken all of their land speed records that they held from WWII. It was as if our servicemen and women were touring the country by way of a cheap travel agency, remember that movie from the 60's "If It Is Tuesday, It Must Be Belgium." Our people did the job that was issued to them. Whether or not they agreed with the U.S. foreign policy, they did it with class and valor. And anyone that has anything bad to say about our military personnel can **KISS MY MONEY MAKING ASS!**

Presently, we still have people in harm's way trying to police the country. We are having young people killed every day trying to help install democracy in the country. Every day on the news, another serviceman/woman has been shot/stabbed/blown up for doing nothing but trying to help these people. Now the U.S. government has figured out a way to bring these murderers to justice. They're offering a $2,500 reward for information leading to an arrest. JUMP BACK JIHAD! I hope we do not bankrupt the federal government by offering such a big reward. Okay civil servants, it's time to get serious about protecting our people. Get serious with the reward money, rules of engagement and protection of our troops or come November 2006, we will get serious in replacing all of you.

General Tommy Franks (CCP # 4 STARS) did an outstanding job winning two campaigns (Afghanistan and Iraq) in such a short time period. Every time you turn on the news, armchair generals were telling the public how bad he was screwing up. Guess what? General Franks was correct. Maybe that was the reason he was still on active duty and they had all retired. General Franks just stepped down from his command and is preparing to retire sometime in the near future. Something he and his wife so justly deserve, but he recently said that American troops were going to be needed in Iraq for a substantial period of time. Where in the U.S. Constitution does it say that we are supposed to be the policing agents of the world?

In February of 2003, my wife and I were on vacation in Hawaii. One night I was watching the evening news when they were showing a Hawaii state senator making a speech on the upcoming war with Iraq. I am sorry I do not recall this man's name, but he made a statement that should be heard by every man, woman, and child in America. Bear with me, because I do not remember it exactly, but you will get the idea. He said something like this:

Why should we trust our government when they are telling us they have the evidence that Iraq has Weapons of Mass Destruction and they're trying to buy nuclear fuel for their bombs and missiles? Are we afraid the government would lie to us? Well, let me give you an example. Thirty years ago, President Nixon told the American public that there were no U.S. military personnel or any military action taking place in Cambodia. When President Nixon gave that speech, I was an Army helicopter pilot who had flown over twenty five missions in Cambodia.

"President Bush, on Wednesday, defended his use of pre-war intelligence on Iraq, saying he is "absolutely confident" in his actions despite the discovery that one claim he made about Saddam Hussein's weapons pursuits was based on false information."[18] As I stated earlier, I was not against making Saddam live up to the agreement that was signed in the early 90's. I just didn't want to put our people in harms way for some trumped up reason.

"Bush did not directly address the misstatement itself, made during his State of the Union address. Instead, he defended his decision to go to war based on a larger body of information. 'There is no doubt in my mind that Saddam Hussein was a threat to the world peace,' the President said. And there's no

---

[18]   Tom Raum, "Bush Defends Use of Iraq Intelligence," Associated Press Writer, <u>Yahoo News</u>, July 9, 2003.

doubt in my mind that the United States did the right thing in removing him from power."[19] My only question is, why did we not remove him in 1991 when his daddy was in office? Was it because OPEC would not allow it? Okay so I lied, that was 2 questions.

"White House spokesman Ari Fleischer set off a furor Monday [July 7, 2003] when, under questioning by reporters, he acknowledged that Bush was incorrect in his State of the Union speech when he said 'The British government has learned that Saddam Hussein recently sought significant quantities of uranium from Africa.' Wednesday, Fleischer said that 'this type of information should not have risen to the level of a presidential speech.' But, he added, 'this is a classic issue of hindsight is 20-20. There's a bigger picture here,' Fleischer told reporters traveling with Bush to South Africa. He repeated administration assertions that Saddam Hussein was trying to reconstitute a weapons of mass destruction program. Other White House officials elaborated on Fleischer's remarks Tuesday, saying the United States had additional evidence of Iraq's nuclear intentions."[20] If the government had this information, then why is it not willing to share it with the citizens? National Security, or is it that we couldn't handle information that is this vital, important, or so complex? Or do they believe the same myth that the news agencies believe, that we are nothing but ignorant masses?

Teddy Roosevelt once said that wars were brought on by old men and resulted in young men being killed. What if there were an international law made that said if countries wanted to go to war, all of their leaders would have to lead at the front lines instead of being hundreds of miles away. How about we give the leader of each government a gun and place both of

---

[19]   Ibid

[20]   Ibid

them in a desert/jungle/downtown/who cares where and let them shoot at each other? Who ever walks away alive, their country wins! Just a thought.

Remember the two clues to know when a politician is lying? It definitely applies here, wouldn't you say? I spoke with several people on the "Right Coast" that were worried about the Weapons of Mass Destruction that Iraq had and they agreed with the invasion plan that the President presented. Now, I want to know how true are the facts regarding North Korea? Remember the "good old days" when Tricky Dickey kept saying "Trust me, I am not a crook!" Kinda makes you stop and go hmmmm...

10.   EDUCATION, OR THE LACK THEREOF

"Integrity without knowledge is weak and useless, and knowledge without integrity is dangerous and dreadful" .... *Samuel Johnson*

On July 20, 1969, as commander of the Apollo 11 lunar module, Neil Armstrong was the first person to set foot on the moon. His first words after stepping on the moon, "That's one small step for man, one giant leap for mankind," were televised to earth and heard by millions. But just before he reentered the Lander, he made the enigmatic remark, "Good luck, Mr. Gorsky." Many people at NASA thought it was a casual remark concerning some rival Soviet cosmonaut. However, upon checking, there was no Gorsky in either the Russian or American space programs. Over the years many people questioned Armstrong as to what the "Good luck, Mr. Gorsky" statement meant, but Armstrong always just smiled.

On July 5, 1995, in Tampa Bay, Florida, while answering questions following a speech, a reporter brought up the 26-year-old question to Armstrong. This time he finally responded. Mr. Gorsky had died, so Neil felt he could answer.

In 1938, when he was a kid in a small Midwest town, he was playing baseball with a friend in the backyard. His friend hit the ball, which landed in his neighbor's yard by the bedroom window. His neighbors were Mr. and Mrs. Gorsky. As he leaned down to pick up the ball, young Armstrong heard Mrs. Gorsky shouting at Mr. Gorsky, "Sex! You want Sex? You'll get sex when the kid next door walks on the moon!"

Educating Young Ccps

With the conditions of most public schools, violence, over crowding, teachers that can't teach and are just giving the students passing grades to get them out of their sphere of influence, buildings in bad conditions, and the general distrust of the public school system, I can understand why parents are home-schooling their children when they can not afford private schools.

What I do oppose is home schooling when the parents themselves have only completed the 9th grade. Remember when your parents screamed at you to turn off the TV and do your homework? Well, today your homework could be watching TV. The airwaves are an equal opportunity educator. Whether you believe in the "Big Bang" theory or Creationism, there is a channel, or a hundred, for you.

You can educate your young ones on everything from the splitting of an Atom to the mating habits of a Zebra and everything in between. Just look at the programs you could schedule for the kids: 0800 The Discovery Channel, 0900 The Learning Channel, 1000 The History Channel, 1100 Internet time for looking up additional information from the previous three channels. See how simple that was? The morning is over before you know it and with over more than 300 channels to choose from, the afternoon could fly by just as quickly. Your child is safe and secure in your own home and could be the next genius of the nation with all of that information bombarding his brain 24 hours a day/7 days a week. Who knows? After two years of TV education, your little one will walk up to you and say, "Mom, after watching the Medical Channel, I feel that I am capable of giving you that breast enhancement and lypo suction procedure you are saving for." What are you going to say to the child prodigy so that you wouldn't dash this budding young surgeon's ego, or further more, scar his psyche for years? More than likely, you would tell the little surgeon about trying something on his/her father and then let me see how it turns out. Just in case the child takes your advice, it might be advisable to have 911 on speed dial. You never know when you could hear a scream coming from your bedroom.

I have an Aunt that received her Associate of Arts degree from a college in Virginia via correspondence courses with video lectures. This took place in the early 90's prior to the Internet boom and this concept was not a bad idea. In this day and age, not only can you receive your AA over the internet, you can earn a Bachelor's Degree and you don't have to stop there! You can go to graduate school via phone line (or for you rich CCPs, a DSL line). Personally, I have nothing against anyone furthering their education by way of the internet, but I will draw the line the day I go into a doctor's offices and see his or her degrees hanging on the wall and they read: Bachelor of Science, School Channel KEZY, and the Doctrine of Medicine, School *WWW.CUTHERE.COM.* Your can bet your happy ass MY ass is not staying in that office long.

Living out here on the left coast for seventeen years, I have observed that life is more laid back and things are done differently than the right coast, but even this is pushing the limits of the imagination. As I mentioned before, my wife is an attorney (boy have I got some great lawyer jokes!), and we are still paying off school loans because she had to attend an accredited law school in order to take the bar exam for the

State of Washington, as well as any of the other state in the Union. Just recently she received an e-mail from one of the law affiliations she belongs to stating that, since Washington has a reciprocal agreement with California, any lawyer graduating from an internet law school that passed the California bar can practice in Washington. As with the doctor's office, if I walk into a lawyer's office and his/her diploma reads Juris Doctorate School of *WWW.SUETHEBASTARD.COM*, I am history.

Today's School

My spelling is so bad that I want to buy the person who invented the spell checker on my computer a drink. As often as I use it, I should pour a drink into the computer, it definitely could use one. I'd like to pay homage to him or her for making my life much easier. In this day and age, when you are typing and you misspell a word, a little red line appears under the word and glares at you until you hit the F7 key, which, by the way, the letter and number are no longer legible on my computer. After hitting that key, a box appears with several suggestions as to the word you are trying to spell and, on some occasions, you will see "no suggestions." When you receive the last statement, you know you have some creative juices flowing. In the process of writing this book, I have typed in some words and gotten that little red line. And when the box appeared, it read, "What the hell are you thinking of?" I guess I have been at the computer a little too long. Either it's trying to read my mind or we have bonded. My favorite statement in the box was after a particularly long word where it read, "Check Webster's; this is above my pay grade."

I always hated when I was younger, and I did not know how to spell a word, my mother or teacher would tell me to look it up in the dictionary. If you don't know how to spell it, how can you look it up in a book? Sound it out phonetically was always the standard answer. That's all well and good for someone that has a clue as to what phonics is. If you had asked me to look up the word phonics in the dictionary, I would have more than likely come up with "Fondness". If you cannot tell by now, English was not my favorite class in school. I was fond of History and P.E., excelled in the latter, of course.

As a whole, our public school systems, let me say this in a PC manner and you know that ain't goanna' happen, **SUCKS!** The kids today coming out of the public systems couldn't find their ass with both hands, even if you had an anatomically correct doll in front of the class. The reason for not finding the correct part is because they cannot read the directions that are printed on the doll's ass. I know, I went to school in the dark ages where we were expected to learn and, if we did not pass our final exams, there were no social promotions, thus insuring our little psyches were scarred for life. You fail? Then your butt stays in the same grade until you pass, or you turn 18 and they kick you out. And teachers actually taught classes. They didn't just take roll call and use the time for study hall. Okay teachers, don't get your panties in a wad, because it's not all your fault.

When did our society start allowing the inmates to run the institution? When little Johnny or Jane could not be punished in school was the start of our schools going to hell in a hand basket. How can we expect teachers to educate our little darlings when they have to worry about their own personal protection and whether they will be sued for hurting little Johnny's feelings? Lord knows we cannot discipline him if he has cussed, hit, or attacked the teacher in his classroom. They shall not spank little Johnny, even through he needs his ass busted. If the little hellion had any pressure applied to his backside, a progressive thinking lawyer would have a multi-million dollar lawsuit filed before the tears quit flowing. June 9, 2003, on the Seattle local news, there was a story about a young boy that was being punished in a time out room. The charming little darling's mother was shown and she stated that this was cruel and unusual punishment. Then they interviewed the principal of the school and they showed the "Time Out" room. It was a 6' x 6' room that was carpeted on the floor as well as the walls. Mommy Dearest claimed this room was something you would find at a mental asylum and was scarring her little darling for life. The principal explained that a teaching assistant should be outside the door (there is a window in the door) talking with the condemned prisoner in the room, asking if he or she is ready to leave the room and assume their proper place in the class room without causing any more disturbances. Now, Mommy finds this a cruel punishment because her little bastard acts up in school and thinks he should be punished in the same manner he is punished at home, which means not a damn thing will happen to him. Here's a thought. Bring Mommy Dearest to the school when little Johnny screws up and sit both of their asses in front of the principal and let Mommy make the choice. Somebody is going to go into the "Time Out" room or get their ass busted. Who is it going to be, and which form of punishment is going to take place? And God knows if we expel little Johnny, here comes another law suit, so the school boards can't win for losing.

When did academia take it upon themselves to "dumb down" our classes so that one child would not have their feelings hurt because they could not keep up with the rest of the class. Lord knows we don't want to reward students that excel in the class. That may give them a superiority complex and motivate them to go forth and be someone worthwhile in their adult life. And we all know when you graduate or get a social promotion from high school, when the young man or woman is given their diploma on the back of that piece of paper is their "Fair Certificate." This certificate will insure that they are treated in the work force in the same manner that they were treated in school. This means if someone is smarter and more motivated on the job, all the recent graduate has to do is flash their "Fair Certificate" to the boss, and the new promotion or pay raise will be theirs, not the person that actually worked for it. The work force will not allow itself to dumb down, but we all know if the government has its way, the work force will get its own version of the dumb down rule.

Testing

This word can create a firestorm just as fast as a pro-choice/pro-life debate. What is the problem with testing? The teacher's union is adamantly against teachers being required to pass a test to teach our children, and their reasoning is that they have a college degree. All of us know people that have a college degree that are dumber than a stump, and you wonder whom they knew or whom they did to earn that diploma. Having a diploma does not automatically certify you with the ability to teach, and the trouble with our colleges that have teaching schools is that they will issue any diploma to students who have finished the curriculum by the skin of their teeth, whether or not they have the ability to teach. Basically, it boils down to money paid, times up, ride is over, get out!

The teachers get all in an uproar when they are required to take the exam to ensure they are competent to teach. I have one question. What makes them think they are better than anybody else in the work force? Oh yeah, I forgot. They obtain **TENURE**, which is another story in and of itself. When I started out working construction, I started in the electrical trade and when I spent my time in school and in the field, I had to take a test. If I passed this test, I received a card stating that I was a Certified Journeyman Electrician. One of my roommates was a pipe fitter/welder, and every project he worked on, before he could weld on the job, he was required to take a welding test. My wife is an attorney and after law school, she was required to take the Bar Exam for the State of Washington, and if she wants to practice (don't you hate it when lawyers and doctors say they are "practicing"; for what they charge you they should have it down pat by now) in any other state, she will be required to pass their bar exam. Doctors are required to pass an exam after school, internship, and residency. What is being said here is that just about every occupation in the work force requires some form of testing that shows the person is capable of being in that position. I have shown where the upper crust of the work force is required to be tested and the middle portion of the work force is tested, so why do teachers think they are any better than the rest of us when we want to be sure that they are capable of teaching our children? I don't know if there is a testing procedure required to flip burgers, but I'm sure they've got to do SOMETHING to earn that little gold crown on their nametag.

Florida's Governor, Jeb Bush, the same guy that issued the paper that ensured that "Chad" got hung in the 2000 November election, has implemented a testing procedure throughout the state, and if a school fails to pass two years in a row, he closes the school and has the children sent to other schools. You have not heard such screaming since the cat got its' tail caught in the fan. Racial discriminating, racial profiling, anti-this and anti-that is being shouted throughout the state. What is not being stated is the truth that some, not all, teachers are not doing their jobs and a majority of the parents that are screaming about discrimination are not doing their jobs, which is to ensure that their little bundles of joy actually attend class and do the class work. But that might mean those parents would actually have to be responsible adults, and we know that isn't going to happen. So what we have here is an endless cycle and when the government steps in, everyone starts crying foul. Trust me, I am not a fan of big government, but there are times that changes need to be made and it usually takes a big stick to make those changes happen.

Tenure

As promised, I am going to discuss one of my favorite topics, tenure. What other profession is out there in the world that, once you reach this certain pinnacle, you can grab this brass ring called tenure and for the rest of your life have a "Get Out of Jail Free" card in the employment world? This day and age, about the only way a teacher is fired is if he or she is having sex with a student. There are cases where teachers have shown up to class under the influence of drugs or alcohol and had to take UA exams and failed. I'm surprised they didn't raise hell about not having enough time to study for the piss test. Even though they didn't pass the test, they could not be dismissed from teaching because they had tenure. Cases of misappropriating funds is not grounds for termination if they have the golden ring called tenure. Maybe this is where the kids learn that there is a "Fair Certificate" in the world. I could ramble on about the subject for hours while truly alienating the majority of the teaching profession, although that is not my intention, but we all know there is a problem in our education system and giving teachers pay raises is not the only cure.

It is our children that we are putting in your care and we expect you to do everything in your power to mold them into responsible adults. And before you start screaming, I agree that yes, it is our responsibility to help in that molding process, but let's look at cold, hard facts. The teachers see the kids more hours per days that most parents. With single parents working two jobs, or in this economy trying to find a job, living is not easy, and as stated earlier "Life is not fair." So whether teachers like it or not, a majority of the responsibility for shaping our children's lives is in their hands.

There is another old saying that everyone has heard and it says, "If it ain't broke, don't fix it." Well guess what, our educational system isn't broke, it's totally collapsed. In industrialized nations, our school system is rated so low it is embarrassing. The U.S. government spends billions of dollars in foreign aid on helping third world nations and their schools. It is time to cut off the faucet to these other countries, and by the way, they do not like us and keep telling us to go home, so let's go home and take our checkbook with us and spend that money on our own school systems. Spend that money on such trivial things like new buildings, maintenance, books, after school functions, computers and pay increases for the teachers that deserve it. Charity should begin at home. Take care of your own family before trying to save the world.

As I stated earlier, I am not the smartest person in the world. I started college in 1970, attended a few years, and then dropped out. In 1995, I graduated from St. Martin's College in Lacey, WA. Okay all you smart asses, I did not attend school all those years straight. Now I am working on my Master's Degree in Engineering Management at the same college. No one has every said an education was easy, and there are people dying around the world because they want an education. For the most part, education in this country is relativity free and people are not taking advantage of it. Okie dokie, I just climbed down off of my soapbox. You didn't know they made them so high, did you? Education is very important to my family, so let's work together to correct the problems in our system.

11.   RHETORIC AND OTHER B.S.

"If you believe in forever then life is just a one night stand" …. Rock' n Roll Heaven… sung by the Righteous Brothers

This chapter is going to be a smorgasbord of miscellaneous matters. These are things that generally tick you off for no particular reason or simply because whatever pissed you off shouldn't have happened. Every CCP has gotten mad enough to bite nails and spit tacks because of some act or lack of action by someone that is taking their money and taking their own sweet time or just being a royal pain in the ass. There are two mottos I conduct business by and they have helped me out on several occasions. Maybe they can help all of my brother & sister CCPs.

1.   If I am paying, I am telling you what I want. If you are paying, you're telling.
2.   Everyone but God has a boss.

Later on in the chapter, I will give you an example of how the second saying has saved my bacon.

Customer Service

When was the last time you went into an establishment that was willing to take your hard earned money, and they have a nice fancy desk that says "Customer Service" and you actually got that service? I am not talking about the usual service where you need a cigarette afterwards and they roll over and go to sleep. I mean, the company actually listens to your problem and does something about it. Was it in the Roman period or the Middle Ages you received satisfaction (no, the Rolling Stones are not a period of history, even though Mick & Keith both look like they were born in the Middle Ages).

In case some managers read this book, please read the next few sentences because I am going to give you the definition of customer service.

1.   **Customer** (kus'ta-mar) 1. One who buys goods or services. 2. A person with whom one must deal.[21]
2.   **Service** (sur'vis) 6. Work done for others as an occupation or business. 11. An act of assistance or benefit. 12. The serving of food or the way in which it is served. 15. Copulation with a female.[22]

It seems that most of the businesses in this country use #15 in the definition of service as the company's mission statement. But what the heck; we now know diversity is working because the companies are equal opportunity fornicators. Big word, huh! And, I do know what it means. Bear with me, for once, I am not being rude, crude, and socially unacceptable. Gender

---

[21]   Riverside Webster's II New College Dictionary, rev. ed. (1995), s. v. "Customer."
[22]   Riverside Webster's II New College Dictionary, rev. ed. (1995), s. v. "Service."

does not matter because everyone is being screwed everyday by business.

Remember back in ancient times when you would go into a hamburger fast food place and their motto was "Have it your way" and they meant it? Now days when you go into one, about the only thing you can get is an attitude. Put down the phone corporate guys, there is no need to call your lawyers. A little constructive criticism never hurt anyone. I am not picking on just you; I am including every other fast food joint in America. You hire a bunch of kids for minimum wage and turn them loose on the public. All of us CCPs know that this is the labor pool that you have to work with, but what we do blame you with is the lack of management. How many times have you walked inside to the counter to place an order and have to wait until the entire staff hears what Buffy is going to wear on her date this weekend or the radical new moves Dr. Death performed on his skateboard at the skateboard park this afternoon? When you walked in there, your child was young enough to order a Happy Meal; by time you placed the order, you have to get it to go because the same child has to catch a plane to go to college.

And don't think the drive-thru is any faster. How many times have you pulled up to the microphone/speaker box to place an order and the quality of the sound is so bad you have no idea what was repeated to you? And to add insult to injury, the clown on the other end of the speaker box is wearing a stud in his or her tongue and then they get pissed when you do not understand them. Once, just once, don't you just want to reach in there and rip that bad boy out of his or her mouth? This would be a case where the Native Americans [PC] had it right with "White man, speak with fork tongue." Then when you are finished haggling at the speaker box, you get to the takeout window and this creature meets you with an attitude. This being has so many body piercings that if it (we are not sure what gender it is and the alien chapter said it is not one of theirs) leans out of the window and the wind is blowing, you will not be able to concentrate due to the whistling sound being emitted from the air rushing through all of the holes in said creatures body. And after you have gone through all of this, when you get home, you find you have half your order and half of someone else. AND WE PUT UP WITH THIS CRAP.

Remember when the major department stores had mottos like "The customer is always right, or "Satisfaction guaranteed" and other silly statements? I am not talking about places like Neiman Marcus, Nordstrom, or any other stores like that because I cannot afford to shop at a place that has a cover charge. I am talking about your every day run of the mill department store, K-Mart, Sears, JC Penney's. This is where the mass of CCPs shop. What happened to service? If you want to return an item, you have to go through a process that makes you feel as if you are being sent to prison. Then the questions are what is wrong with it? Why don't you want it? Why don't we start acting just as rude as some of these "customer service" employees in answering their questions? What's wrong with it? It doesn't work and it's a piece of crap! Why don't you like it? It looks like something you would wear and I would not be seen at a wrestling match wearing it! It is none of their business why I do not want the item. All I want from them is a smile, a "yes sir" (this would be really stretching it) and a refund or exchange. Maybe some of these big name companies should shop Wal-Mart on a regular basis and maybe something would rub off on them, because Wal-Mart is doing something correct.

This is the example of "Everyone but God has a Boss." Back in the 90's, I built a house and I was the contractor for the project, thus I was in charge of getting all of the materials and insuring it was shipped to the house. My family was preparing to move into the new house a few days before Christmas. As everyone knows, the holidays involve a great amount of cooking, and cooking requires an oven and a stove. I had purchased all of my kitchen appliances at Sears because everyone knows their Kenmore line is outstanding. The only problem I had was the local store had sent the wrong stove out to my new house three previous times. On the fourth delivery it was the same stove that had been sent on trips two and three. Being the calm, cool person that I am (trust me this was a strain because I was so mad I could have bit nails and spit tacks), I calmly walked away from the delivery truck and called the store and spoke with the shipping manager. I explained to him the problem and that I needed the stove since it was Christmas Eve and I had people coming over. He proceeded to tell me, in a very condescending voice, that the store was having its Christmas party and there would be no one that would be available to deliver the stove. I asked him to transfer me to the appliance manager, which he did. I explained the situation to the appliance manager and he gave me the same story about a Christmas party. I asked the appliance manager to transfer me to the store manager, which he happily did. When the store manager got on the line I explained the story for the third time, and he explained to me, in the same voice and tone the shipping manager had, about the Christmas party and added that the stove would be delivered December 26th. When I asked for Sears home office's telephone number in Chicago, he asked me to verify my address and the stove would be at my house in two hours. As much as I wanted to scream and cuss at these people, that one lesson my father had taught me worked well. And it has worked well over the years. Everyone but God has a boss.

Obesity and Cars

I know the majority of you are probably asking yourselves, "How the heck are obesity and cars related?" Just bear with me and I will show you. As stated previously I know I am overweight. I am 6'8" tall and weight 275 pounds. I weigh 10 pounds more than when I was playing ball, but trust me, the package does not look the same and gravity has shifted everything to the middle. How many times have you heard on the nightly news (and if you read the news chapter it is up to you whether or not you believe them) that the government's statistics shows 50, 60, 70, 80, 90 percent of the American population is obese. The U.S. standards for being overweight are just as asinine as the majority of their other rules and regulations. No wonder they pay $500 for a hammer and a $1,000 for a toilet seat when purchasing items for government contracts. Brother and Sister CCPs, go on the Internet and look up the U.S. standard for being overweight. It is truly amazing how ridiculous the charts are. If everyone believed these charts, then Arnold Schwarzenegger would be in the obese category along with the majority of centerfolds that have appeared in Playboy. We all know that silicon is heavy, but this is ridiculous! Now I know where all the models go to work when age catches up with them and they can no longer be one of the "Beautiful People." They become civil servants for the federal government working in the department that deals with weights and measurement standards. Going by the governments standards, at 245 lbs I am still overweight. I would have to weight 225 lbs. to not be considered overweight by the brain trust of the U.S. government. At 225, I would look like a person being released from a concentration camp. I know I weighed 225 lbs. one time in my life; I did not just jump to 275. But trust me it wasn't a pretty site to see someone 6'8" and all bones. I think the people developing these weird standards are the same guys who have convinced their girlfriends/wives/significant others that the space between these two brackets is really six inches [--------------]. Then again, that last little misinformation fact could bring on a whole chapter regarding the rhetoric that male CCPs have spoken to female CCPs. However, I would have to research this deeply since I have never misled a female CCP in any way shape or form.

Now watch closely. Here is where obesity and cars tie in, and it happens so elegantly, even if I do say so myself. With all of the government standards being issued, why are the cars getting smaller? If we are becoming a society of fat asses, why are the car manufacturers building cars that will only accommodate one cheek of these fat asses? Hold on before you come unglued and start screaming at me about all of the trucks and SUVs on the road. The primary word in the previous sentence was **car**. And the primary culprit of this shrinking car dilemma is the Japanese car manufacturers'. Just because their economy has been shrinking since the 1990's, it does not mean their cars should follow.

The first import I had was a 1981 Datsun 280 Z and it was the first car I had ever owned that went over one hundred thousand miles. I know all of you have a funny look on your face imagining me in that little car, but believe it or not, I could sit upright in the seat and stretch my legs out completely straight and go fast. And did I mention it would go really fast? Then I traded it in for a 1985 Nissan 300 ZX and still had plenty of room and it would go really fast and from there it has gone downhill. Try to get into a sports car today if you are over five feet nothing - you won't fit. What is wrong with the Japanese? Don't they believe our government statistics that Americans are getting bigger and fatter? We are their biggest trading partner. If they do not retool their industry, the market is literally going to outgrow them. Then what we will have to buy, British cars? We all know they are about as reliable as a U.S. built car.

I know I just pissed off a good number of CCPs with that last statement, but U.S. car manufacturers do not even know the meaning of quality control and here are my personal facts to support that statement. Since 1981, I (or someone in my immediate family) have owned a Japanese import, and the total number would be seven with every vehicle going over 150,000 miles. My wife's first Toyota Celica had over 245,000 miles on it when a power company truck crashed into it and totaled it. With all of these vehicles combined, I had less than $3,500 in repairs (barring standard maintenance such as changing oil, etc.). Since 1997, feeling un-American, I have bought two red, white, and blue flag- waving vehicles. The first was a Jeep Cherokee and the second was a GMC Jimmy. Yes, I am into SUVs since I can't fit into their cars and two of my imports were SUVs. The jeep was painted red and it was affectingly known in our family as the "Red Lemon." The vehicle was purchased in Mobile, AL and, while driving across country to Washington, three transfer cases had to be installed and that was just the beginning. We had a pool going on in the family if the vehicle would last 100,000 miles. I kept the vehicle long enough to win the pool and at 101,000, traded it in. Still feeling patriotic, I purchased the Jimmy and since it is black we lovingly refer to it as the "Black Hole." It just hit 100,000 miles and its days are numbered. What I am trying to tell you in this last bit of rambling is that I have spent twice the amount of money on two vehicles than I did on the other seven combined. Whatever happened to the idea of taking pride in your work, or maybe just a little bit of quality control from the Big three would be nice.

Here's a thought. Why doesn't Detroit import some Japanese engineers and quality control inspectors and drain their brains? In turn, we know the Japanese will be copying all our size and measurements for vehicles and take this knowledge back home, thus making bigger cars and the world would be a happier place. Just think, CCPs would have a choice. An American made vehicle that would last and not cost an arm and leg to operate, or a Japanese import that did not come equipped with a shoe spoon to help pry your butt in and out of the seat.

T-Shirts

If you are going to wear a T-shirt with a logo or statement, at least believe in the product. All CCPs can respect you for that whether on not we agree with what is printed on the shirt. But if it is an out and out lie or maybe a far-fetched fantasy, you should not wear it and here is a good example:

I was working on a project in Pennsylvania and was in a grocery store one evening. As I was walking down an aisle, I noticed a man at the far end of the aisle with a six-pack of beer in his hands (true CCP). He looked like the typical biker with a Harley T-shirt, scraggly beard, boots, but he was wearing cut off shorts. Around his big calf (this guy was my size) he had a tattoo going around his leg. My first thought was that it would be the type that looks threatening, like barbwire. But no, to my amazement, as he got closer he had all of the cartoon characters from the Bugs Bunny show. You know Daffy, Foghorn, Pepe Le Pew, Sylvester and the rest of the gang. Let me tell you! Seeing those tattoos just made fear run rampant throughout my body! Oh wait. Maybe it was uncontrollable laughter that I had mistaken for fear. After seeing this sight, I cut my shopping short to see what type of "HOG" this guy was riding. Trust me, I did not want to provoke this guy because anyone that would show that tattoo in public was either one mean son of a bitch or a crazy one. Either way I did not want to mess with him. Once he got into the parking lot, he walked over to where there were three bikes parked, and to my amazement, he got onto a beat up old HONDA. His CCP card has since been revoked. You cannot find truth in advertising anywhere.

Al Basher, the brewmaster from Noah's ark, told me about a T-shirt he bought while visiting his daughter that lives in

Texas. Now this is one shirt that I would say has a lot of truth in it. "MY ANGER MANAGEMENT GROUP IS STARTING TO REALLY PISS ME OFF!" Need I say more?

Models and Women's Fashion

Where on God's green earth do these fashion designers come up with the ideas for some of the clothes they show in public? And once they spring these creations on the public, how do they get their initial investments back, much less a profit? I know these clothes cost tens of thousands of dollars, but how many do they actually sell, since most women that buy designer clothes want an original and they do not want to show up at a party with all of the other beautiful people and find some other Diva wearing her dress. And if they're the beautiful people, does that make us the ugly ones? Anyway, for all of us lowly people that see glimpses into this world when they show the new fashions on the news, it looks like a big-time expensive show. I would like to see the way the designers get the return on their money. This is one huge money making industry and I am just too slow to understand how all of it works.

What CCP female, and in some cases male, can afford these creations, and if they took out a second mortgage on the home to pay for it, where would you be brave enough to be seen in public wearing this marvelous outfit? One thing you can be sure to bet the ranch on is that you will never see any of these creations in Wal-Mart or Kmart. Bear with me in this fantasy; if by some chance some of these clothes were sent to Wal-Mart or Kmart, either by court order or because someone has a picture of the designer and a goat in a compromising position, who is going to buy these? There is no way they will fit anyone that is older than 3.

Have you taken a good look at the models that they use on these "runways"? I weighed more at birth than most of these ladies. And where in the real world do you see women this size? When the average American woman wears a size 10 (it may actually be larger but if you think I want 100 million women pissed at me, you are on drugs), why don't these designers make clothes that would fit these women? If they would put labels in the clothes saying they were a size 10 but in reality they were 12/14, the designers would be billionaires. I am not trying to tell these people how to do their jobs, but everyone could use a helping hand every now and then.

E-Mail Spam & Pop Up Ads

I truly believe when President Bush was giving the American public a roll call of the players in the "Axis of Evil" he forgot to mention a few. The people who flood your e-mail with spam should be added to that list. And the people that developed the pop-up ads should be on the known terrorist list that the Department of Homeland Security has in place. From now on, these people that have developed and sent this trash to your computers will be known lovingly as CAs (Commercial Asses). I did say that lovingly. When captured, CAs should be sent to the prison located at Guantanamo Bay, Cuba and when it comes time for their release, their release papers should be sent out via the Internet. Although personally, I think they should get life and a day. This would ensure it would take a long time for all of the correct paper work to come through because the person at the prison would have to go through at least a month of spam before they got to the release papers. I believe that the CAs who developed spam and pop-up ads are the same people that developed the software to block these royal pains in the asses and are willing to sell it to you for the low price of $19.95. Speaking of, have you ever noticed how many items you can buy at the low, low price of $19.95? I think I can smell a conspiracy here. And have you noticed the blocking software is just one-step or version behind the spam or ads? I rest my case.

How many of you have actually bought something from spam or a pop-up ad on the Internet? How many of you are brave enough to say in public that you have bought something from one of these creatures that are spawned in Hell? If Dante would have had a computer and was connected to the Internet, he would have made spam/pop-ups one of the Rings of Hell. Maybe these CAs are people that were placed in the Witness Protection Program, because you have never seen or heard of one of these people. Ex-mobsters and drug kingpins would make excellent employees since their previous employment was making everyone else's life a living hell. I checked with the alien chapter to see if these CAs were from their group and they assured me they were not because all of their CAs were vaporized ions ago and no one was brave enough to try it again. You have to admit, their idea is better than Cuba.

How do these people get paid? Is it by the number of responses from their evil creation? Once a person responds by trying to get their e-mail address off their mailing list, does that automatically add them to a telemarketer's call list? Which by the way is another ring of Dante's Hell. That has to be it: the spam company is making a list of customers and they sell the list to the telemarketers because they cannot be making any money from their ads. I believe the government should take stronger action in curtailing this cruel and unusual punishment. My idea is for every hacker and/or virus inventor that is in jail to spend all of their time developing software that would send the spam or pop-up ads back to the CAs, thus creating a loop and overloading their machines. Then we alert the Department of Homeland Security to alert the neighborhood watches to be watching for small explosions that would be brought on by the computer overloads. Once the CAs are identified, then they could be transported to Cuba. I am in favor of allowing the alien chapter to be in charge of transportation. By doing it this way, we wouldn't have to worry about overcrowding in the prisons!

FDA Reduces Food Warning Levels

The FDA has come up with a new chart showing how healthy the food you are about to eat is. They like the color chart that the Homeland Security Department came up with, and they were not going to be out done, so they came up with this cute little A, B, C, D ratings. Here we go again, not only is the federal government going to educate us, now they are going to grade us. Until today, the Food and Drug Administration has issued the rules and regulations that were very strict regarding what companies claimed to be health benefits on their labels. Before a product could state health benefits (heart-healthy, low cholesterol, etc) there had to be significant scientific results proving their claims, but not anymore. Under this new plan that starts September 1, 2003, the FDA will allow certain foods to make "qualified health claims" in the same manner that the courts have allowed for the loosely (that's an understatement) regulated dietary supplements.

Congressman Henry Waxman, D-CA, stated the following, "FDA's decision is going to permit virtually unsupported health claims on foods. When consumers see a claim on a product and later learn it was a false claim, they're going to decide perhaps none of the labels on those food products mean anything." The FDA Commissioner, Mark McClellan, said "Americans shouldn't need a science degree to figure out how foods can fit into a healthy diet, and they are presently bombarded with nutrition information that the claims rankings will help them sort out. Information should be accurate, honest and easy to understand."

With all of that hot air, I mean rhetoric, spouted, here is the new information the government is allowing on food labels to make it easier for the masses to understand what they are eating and what effect it will have on them twenty years from now.

New Rating You Will See On Packages

1. For scientifically proven claims
2. The science is good but not conclusive
3. There is limited science to support a claim
4. There are hardly any scientific studies on this product.

The New Ratings You Will Not See On Packages

1. Everyone but the government and consumers are getting rich on this one
2. Find anything healthy here and you are using a microscope
3. Going to make more money than the law should allow
4. Hide the money in an off shore bank
5. I want this lobby group working for me in the future
6. Just in case someone gets sick, skip the next rating and go to L
7. Kill/death/coma. Go to next rating
8. Lawyers telephone numbers
9. Money makes the world go around; especially in DC

10. Never met a politician that could not be properly lobbied
11. Opportunity knocks once. Cash in quickly
12. PROFIT! Need I say more?
13. Quality control is found in fairy tales
14. Really, really bad product but you will still buy it
15. Stock Options, financial security deposited in Cayman
16. Time bomb - by the time the lawsuits start the company will be defunct
17. USA - where a single idea can make you a billionaire
18. Value? You can't be serious! Be happy it doesn't kill you.
19. Wake me up, I cannot believe how much money we are making
20. X-rayed food, or, was it stored at Three Mile Island?
21. You cannot believe how easy it was to get this changed
22. ZZZZZ Someone was sleeping to let this one go through

Just remember those famous words "We are the government and we are here to help you." Just be thankful they did not end the announcement with "Trust Us." Sleep tight tonight, your government is watching out for all of us. Or, is that, they are *watching* us; who knows, they are doing something.

Movie Reviewers

When are the television channels, newspapers and magazines going to hire some reviewers that know what the average CCP wants to watch? How many times have you seen this

Professional Movie Goer (PMG) review a movie you have been waiting to see and in their review, they want you to sign up for a class action lawsuit so you can get your money back. And then you go to the movie reluctantly (not really; it's your significant other that does not want to go, but you saw at least four explosions in the preview) only to find out that it was the best movie you have seen in the past six weeks. Personally, I've found that when the PMG does not like the movie, that is a sure sign of four thumbs up for a good number of CCPs, and myself. I do not know about the majority of you, but I go to the movies to be entertained, escape from reality, or just to have fun. I do not go to be educated, and as it is well documented in earlier chapters, we all know that I am just one step out of the "Iron Age." And the artsy films - give me a break! The people that go to these movies are the same ones that attend the opera. Then they come out of the opera talking to everyone with an attitude as if they understood what the hell the actor was singing about. Let's get in the real world here. You can get your every day male CCP to go to a chick flick a hell of a lot faster than you can get him to go to an artsy film. And why is that you ask? Simple... he may have a chance of getting laid after the chick flick, but the odds on getting lucky with an artsy film is with the house.

My question is, how can one person know what everyone likes? I know some of these PMGs have gotten in touch with their feminine side, and the majority have forgotten to take their testosterone pills prior to going into the theater when the movie was made for us knuckle dragging, beer swilling, meat eating, unsociable, insensitive men. Or yet, go to an animated film and do a review that a kid does not have the slightest idea of what was just said about the movie. Society put a great amount of pressure on the movie industry back in the 1960's to introduce the rating systems. You know what I'm talking about: G, PG-13, R, and X (least we forget the ones that you definitely do not want anyone seeing you going into or out of the theater). Well I am suggesting something in the same manner, but here is where I could get into trouble with the EEOC.

If a movie is in the Action Classification, (definition of action is 1) more than one explosion, 2) more than two chase scenes car, boat, horses, copter - who cares, 3) more than fifty bullets in the air during the first five minutes) it will be reviewed by a male that is not in touch with their feminine side, or, to be fair to the other sex, a female that is in touch with her male side. Or, in the famous words of Robin Williams, "Women who wear comfortable shoes." If this PMG gets squeamish at eating a rare steak, that would be grounds for termination. Hell, the majority of us male CCPs want a PMG that would cover our six in a firefight. If they don't know what covering your six or fire fight means, that is grounds for termination. And don't think all of us knuckle draggers don't mind a love story being in the middle of the movie. That is the only way our significant others would even consider riding in the same vehicle with us to the movie, plus we all know a little T&A always adds spice to the movie.

Here is the rating system for action movies:

1. **1 Hand Grenade:** Any action movie (see definition above)
2. **C-4:** John Travolta films (The General's Daughter, Basic, etc)
3. **Smart Bomb:** Mel Gibson movies
4. **Bunker Buster:** Bruce Willis movies
5. **Nuclear Bomb:** Arnold's movies (if you do not know which Arnold I am talking about, you belong in the next PMG reviewer group)

The "Chick Flicks" classification films (every movie made that does not fit the "action" definition) definitely need to be reviewed by a female or someone that is in touch with their feminine side. Most of today's PMGs could keep their jobs by reviewing only these films. Most male CCPs would rather have a root canal done without pain killers than go to one of these films, but we male CCPs are like Pavlov's dog; we are trainable. We male CCPs know that if there is a good two hanky "Chick Flick" that our significant other wants to see, we will go because we know if we don't, the odds on us having sex in the next two quarters of this year are... well, let's put this in terms men can understand. You have better odds of winning the Lotto without purchasing a ticket. And when a male CCP sees another male CCP in a "Chick Flick," eye contact will never be made, nor will they acknowledge the presence of each other, but you can bet your ass they will tell their buddies that they saw "Old So & So" going into the theater that was playing a "Chick Flick."

Here is the rating system for Chick Flicks:

1. **One Handkerchief:** Old Yellar dies
2. **Two Handkerchief:** Bambi's mother dies
3. **Box of Kleenex:** A really good, if there is such a thing, Chick Flick
4. **Paper Towel Dispenser from the Restroom:** Outstanding Chick Flick (bear with me on the last two ratings since I do not have a large resource pool regarding chick flicks, nor am I willing to research the matter to correct my lack of chick flick knowledge)

Kids' films should be reviewed by kids! Not by some old man who has forgotten what it was like to be a kid. Or some other PMG who thinks they are cool enough to understand what kids like today. Have the PMGs kids or grandkids write the reviews for these films. By doing this, maybe the kids will not want to go, thus saving the parents time and money. Key word here is time. How many times have you taken the kids to some dumb movie that you had to sit there with them, only to hear them say they didn't like it? Let the kids talk to the kids about these movies; it will save on the wear and tear of your nerves. Since I have even less resources regarding children's movies than chick flicks, I will show the new rating system starting with the lowest rating going to the highest.

Here is the rating system for kid's films:

1. **A Box of Popcorn**
2. **A Box of Candy**
3. **A Box of Candy with a Large Soda**
4. **Glucose with IV Needle attachment** (the ultimate sugar high - guaranteed not to sleep for three days)

Grocery/Department Store Chaos

What law of physics is it that deals with shopping carts? When you walk into the store, you are faced with the dilemma that every CCP has faced in their lifetime. Ain't tradition great? Which shopping cart do I choose? You can look at five or six rows of carts, you can call in your locale mechanic and have him/her inspect the cart and just as sure as God makes little green apples, when you get to the back of the store, the wheels will start making a loud noise or pulling to the left. This is where the law of physics comes into play because you have passed the point of no return - and what is this you ask? It is the point where the cart is too full and it is to far away from the front of the store to go back and get a new cart, so you continue pushing a cart that is making a loud obnoxious noise that makes everyone look at you with that "you poor deprived child" look. Or they look at you as if you were drunk, because the minute you let go of the cart it takes an immediate turn into a display case in the middle of the aisle.

Why is it that when you see a homeless person pushing a cart on the street, their cart operates perfectly? If a homeless person can keep up the maintenance on their cart, you'd think the multimillion-dollar corporations could spend a little cash for upkeep on their vehicles. I am sure somewhere in America some lawyer is lurking down an aisle waiting for someone to show signs of SCSS (Shopping Cart Stress Syndrome), and get them to sign up with three other customers so a billion dollar class action lawsuit can be filed. Well, I covered the vehicles and how well they are maintained, now let's discuss the idiots that drive these wonderful inventions.

Have you ever noticed how people that drive these carts have a direct relationship into the manner of which they drive their cars? How many times have you followed some idiot in traffic that is speeding, changing lanes without warnings, much less a signal, and that same person pulls into the store parking lot two cars ahead of you? Yep, all of that hard work really paid off helping them to get the pole position didn't it? They go into the store almost in a full run and grab the first cart they see. Whether it is full or not is of no concern to them; it may have some items they want. If not, they will leave them on shelves throughout the store, including the small child that was sitting in the seat when they got the cart. They race through the aisles as if their asses were on fire and they expect everyone to get out of their way. Being the rude, crude, socially unacceptable person that I am, I have been known to put a speed bump or two in front of these people. Drop a mop in front of the cart and watch how fast they come to a halt. After they climb out of the front of the cart and say a few discouraging words, they do have a tendency to slow down, at least around you.

Then you have the people that think the store is a social gathering place or somewhere to hold family meetings, high school/college reunions in the middle of an aisle or just inside the door making everyone else go around them. A little trick I've learned is to use your cart as a battering ram and go through them at full speed, and as you pass through them, be sure to say, "Excuse You". A) It is not yours, B) No insurance is required! When you glance back, you will be met with a look of confusion because they cannot believe what you just did, and they think you were polite while doing it. How many times have you turned a corner and almost run into one of these reunions taking place, slamming on brakes so hard that you almost threw little Johnny/Sally out of the cart because they were standing up in the seat of the cart in clear violations to the rules that are posted on the carts by direct orders of the company's legal department? The next time you come up on one of the reunions, scream at the top of your lungs "Kirk to Scotty, Scotty give me all the power you can because we are going to ram them!!" If you don't think they will scatter like quail, just watch. Either they'll think you are crazy or that maybe you are from California and you really do know Scotty.

The other mentally handicapped/removed/or plain stupid cart driver that hits my hot button is the person that will leave their cart in the middle of one aisle, and I do mean the middle, so everyone has to jockey around it with their full carts, while they are three aisles over shopping. First of all, that is why they put wheels on the damn carts, so you can take them with you. But, oh no! The people come back from their expedition three aisles over with their arms full of merchandise, and just before they get to the cart, they drop a jar of Mayonnaise. Have you ever tried to clean up a full jar of Mayonnaise? The store should be allowed to have the stock person legally shoot this idiot, therefore ensuring the gene pool is drained just a little, thus ensuring the stock person's children will not have to clean up after a future family member of this idiot.

I truly love watching the elderly drive these carts while shopping, and the following is broken down by gender. The elderly female driver will take her time inspecting everything she is going to purchase, comparing prices, quantity, size, weight, etc., and all the while is dressed as if she was going to a church social. Sometimes these little ladies are carrying on conversations with people that are not visible to you (but what the heck; whom am I to say someone is not with them) and they are having a grand old time. The men go through the aisles just pitching items in the cart like every male CCP from the beginning of time has done - old habits die hard. Then they go over to the frozen food aisle and watch the young ladies wearing halters or bathing suit tops come down the aisle. Some of these men have been known to talk to themselves, but if you get close enough, you will hear the conversation is actually taking place between the old man and his "Johnson," reminiscing about days gone by and what they could do if they were fifty years younger.

Alas, all good things must come to an end, and now you must check out. No matter what lane you pick, the entire 101st airborne division of the army will have gone through the other lanes by the time you get up to the checker. And just as sure as the sun comes up in the east, you are going to get the checker that is bound and determined that every item will be read by the bar code scanner, come hell or high water. How many times have you seen a checker run an item across a scanner 10 or 12 times and then look up at you like it is your fault that it will not read? I'll admit I have used a pen to add some lines to the bar code. But that's another story. God forbid they will have to input the UPC number in by hand. And of course, one item has not been entered into the computer, so there is no price registering and they call out to the slowest employee in the store to go to the back of the building to get the price, and by time they return, the ice cream that has been checked is melted, and the milk is now buttermilk. You do not have to worry about someone stacking cans on top of your bread anymore because most of these places do not have enough stock boys and girls to help all of the lanes of checkout so you end up bagging your stuff with a disgruntled checker.

The next checkout experience I truly love is going into the "EXPRESS LANE" that is reserved for 15 items or less. This is a true lesson on the sad state of our educational system in this country, because the majority of these people do not know how to count or they do not know the definition of "less." All of you have heard stories about scientists conducting experiments on mice by using electric currents, and the mice learn from these shocking experiences. If we can teach mice, are you telling me humans are dumber than rats? Think about this training aid. It would be successful, and violators would only need one lesson and I assure you they would not show back up in the "Express Lane" to violate the 15 items rule.

First, in front of the counter there will be a steel plate that the shopper stands on and behind the counter the checker will have a rheostat, which is a dimmer switch for lights or fans that controls an electrical current. The rheostat will be turned down to zero as the shopper approaches, if the checker sees 16 items in the cart, the switch is turned up and a mild charge is going through the steel plate basically giving the shopper a "Hot Foot." If the shopper has 17 items in the cart, the switch is turned up another notch, thus making every hair on the shoppers body stand straight out, thus ensuring every shopper in the check out lanes notice this person violated the rules and will require a day at the beauty shop to recover. 18 items in the cart and the power is turned up enough to bring on muscle cramps, thus making the violators pee on themselves. 19 items will bring on a current severe enough to make the violator fall to the ground into the fetal position swearing they will never come through that lane again. 20 or more items and the power will be turned up enough to blast their ass to the parking lot, thus ensuring they will never walk through the hallowed halls of this building again. Now tell me they would not learn the first time they came through Mary Ann's Express Lane check out.

I know that there are hundreds of other things that generally tick all of us CCPs off every day. And no matter how much we complain, yell, scream, cuss or cry, nothing is going to change if we do it individually. That is where the CCPP could come into play. Not only can it be a political party, but also it can act as a consumer protection agency. Remember the silent majority that Old Tricky Dickey kept referring to? Well, that showed one thing...keeping quiet did not help him. There is a verse in the Bible that states "The meek shall inherit the earth" but the loud mouths won't have to wait for someone to die off to take over. There are other sayings such as the squeaky wheel gets the grease, etc., etc., etc. We do not have to be timid or act alone to make changes and the one saying that proves that is "Money Talks and Bullshit Walks." If all the CCPs work together, changes can be made non-violently and for the better of everyone. Think about it, it could work.

12.   POLITICAL CORRECTNESS

I have a dog's attitude on life and that is, if you can't eat it, drink it, or screw it, piss on it! ....
Tony Cotton

How about that for a politically correct statement? The "Politically Correct Police" are holding a wildcat strike and have walked out of the building. While they are gone, I am writing this chapter and will hide it until it goes to print. The majority of us are getting fed up with all of these enlightened people telling us how we should think and talk. God knows we would not want to offend someone. I mean if we offend that person, her/his psyche maybe scarred for life. And how can society live with itself if someone goes home tonight without that warm and fuzzy feeling that we all get from being held close to the bosom of "Politically Correct Utopia?" Did that last question convince you that I have seen the light and have left my old rude, crude, knuckle dragging Neanderthal ways of life? If you believe that B.S. then you also believe that George Bush and Ted Kennedy are looking out for your best interest.

This chapter is going to show you some of the most asinine statements printed or spoken in regards to being politically correct. If you are still reading this chapter after plodding through the first two chapters, you know by now I do not give a rat's ass for the politically correct movement that is going through the country. And if I hurt your fragile psyche for not being politically correct here are a few options: 1) close the book and give it away, 2) close the book and burn it, 3) continue reading the book, or 4) or kiss my unpolitically-correct ass. For some reason my mother always tells people the only use for tact I have is putting something up on a bulletin board. What do you think she means by that?

What Is This World Coming To?

Sometime during President Clinton's administration, one of the government officials made a speech in which he used the word "Niggardly." There was such an uproar from "Politically Enlightened" you would have thought he was a convicted child molester that was running a daycare. How dare he come close to using the N-WORD! Why would the Clinton administration allow such an uneducated, rude, crude moron to appear in public, much less make a speech. Obviously, thousands, if not millions of young psyches would be scarred for life. If these critics had their way, this gentleman would have been the first person to be publicly executed in approximately fifty years. And the sad part is that the Clinton administration bowed to these pompous Dumb Asses. I tried to find the gentleman's name and the department he worked in but was unable to come up with the information. All I know is that at the time the story took place, it pissed me off (along with a multitude of people). For all of the enlightened ones that called for his head, since you obviously do not know how to read a dictionary, I will take a little time to try to enhance your enlightenment.

Niggardly: adj. 1. Not willing to spend, give, or share: 2. Scanty: meager. **–nig'gard.li.ness** n. **–nig'gard.ly** adv.[23]

Now for all of you enlightened people, don't you feel so much better now that I have added to your education. Just remember that old saying "A mind is a terrible thing to waste".

LA LA Land (A.K.A. Los Angeles)

On November 24, 2003, an announcement came out of the Office of Diversity (or whatever the dumbass office that issued the memo is) that stated the city would not tolerate vendors/ contractors to use the terms "Masters and Slaves" when describing a group of computers or PLCs (Programmable Logic Controllers) that are working together in series. It seems this terminology is offensive to some of the city's employees. If these employees were former slaves, shouldn't they be retired by now? I know it takes an act of Congress to get rid of some of these civil servants, but this is ridiculous. I have done business with the city of L.A. and some of these people move as if they are 140 years old, but this is taking the "PC" movement to a new height.

I have worked in the electrical industry for over twenty-five years and the practice of designating one computer as the "Master" and the additional computers as "Slaves" is the universal term and is the SOP (Standard Operating Procedure). So now anyone doing electrical or I.T. work in La La Land will have to learn new terminology when working with multiple computers. The only problem with this new scenario is the "Enlightened Person" that created this dumb frigging memo did not give any suggestions as to what to call the computers so bear with me as I make a few suggestions.

---

[23] Webster's II New College Dictionary, (Houghton Mifflin Company Publisher, 1995), 738.

OLD NAME: Master / Slave
NEW NAME:

1. Enlightened One / Dumbass
2. Bureaucrat / Other Useless Bastards
3. Head Honcho / Peons
4. Omnipotent / Impotent
5. Have / Have Nots
6. Republicans / Democrats (This one changes automatically if the power base shifts in Congress)
7. John Wayne / The Calvary
8. The Idiot that wrote the memo / The population of L.A.

Like I said, these are only a few suggestions, so feel free to add to the list. Why is it that California gives the country the majority of these stupid laws/orders? The majority of the time, the population of the remaining forty nine states just stand around scratching their watches and winding their asses to see what will come out of California next.

Classification Of A Group Of People

One day I was in my wife's law office when she asked me to come in and answer some questions about Louisiana. The reason she asked me in was due to the fact that I had lived and worked in the state for three years in the early 80's prior to meeting her. She had another lawyer in the office with her and he was from Seattle. I knew the gentleman (I am using that term loosely when describing a lawyer) for a number of years and let me tell you he is the most politically correct person in the United States. This big city lawyer is a walking advertisement for "Political Correctness", and the following are his qualifications: He looks as if he is a male model and his clothes look as if they have been seen in issues of GQ. He is a Republican and he is gay (don't you know that last statement just puckered Rush Limbaugh's ass?).

I had worked in the area he had some business transactions taking place, and he asked me some questions about the people he would be dealing with. The first thing I told him was that if he came off as some big city lawyer those Coon Asses would eat him alive. You would have thought I had kicked him in the family jewels when I said the words "Coon Asses." He began to preach to me about my caveman ways. How could I possibly talk so negatively about any group of people in this day and age? He was so upset he started to hyperventilate. Jeannie (my wife) had to make him sit down and put his head between his legs to catch his breath. I tried to explain to him that the people of Louisiana that were of French decent took pride in the term "Coon Ass." And when I told him that a group of these people where known as "R.C.A's". He got a very perplexed look on his face and asked, "What is a RCA?" I informed him that if the Coon Asses in question's parents were Coon Asses, and that makes him/her a "Registered Coon Ass", meaning they had papers proving they are certified Coon Asses. Well that statement sent him over the edge. He grabbed his chest and hit the floor. My wife hit the ground and started performing CPR and told me to start giving him mouth-to-mouth resuscitation. I don't know about the majority of you, but the only lawyer I am going to lay my lips on is my wife, so I promptly left the room. The last I heard, he recovered and is still in Seattle but he avoids me like the plague.

People Of Color

If I stood in the middle of a mall and was making a speech and described a man/woman/child as a "Colored Person," the Politically Correct Police would pull me off the stage. Next they would strap me to a cross and brand me with a big red "R" in the middle of my forehead, announcing to the world that I am a racist. Now let's back up in time (who says time travel is not possible?) and in that same speech I had called that man/woman/child a "Person of Color." Now the only thing I did was switch the position of the two nouns and add a preposition. Hallelujah! I have now become one of the enlightened ones. I can walk through the hallowed halls of Utopia, knowing I have not offended anyone today. Now tomorrow is a different story. Why is it that all of the politicians have to categorize everyone in a certain little box? Didn't that piece of paper that was written hundreds of years ago that we base the majority of our laws on state this? I know you all have heard of it, the US Constitution. I like the part where it says everyone is created equal (let's see the PC police jump my ass for that last sentence).

As you know by now, my wife is an attorney, and we live in a small town. It is so small that it has only one street light and a traffic jam is three pickup trucks loaded with hay driving down Main Street. She was appointed to be the Municipal Court Judge by the Mayor of said hole in the wall. This Court meets on the first Friday of the month, and my wife would sit on the bench and listen to all of the defendants as to why they were speeding. "I wasn't as drunk as the officer claims", "I did not beat her with a hammer, I just used a bottle," along with a host of other violations. But prior to sitting on the bench, she attended "Judges College" for approximately a week. This college is given every year to teach new judges what the rules and procedures are according to the laws of the State of Washington. Around the end of the course, the instructors held a class on "Diversity" and it revolved around the issue regarding People of Color and People of Non-Color.

Prior to meeting my wife, I was a shy, quiet, introverted person. Since I have been with her all of these years I have become an extroverted and opinionated man. Okay, I am back; my wife just knocked me silly after reading that last sentence over my shoulder. Maybe I did have some of those traits before I met her. Ouch! Okay, Okay, I had a lot of those traits before I met her (now go away honey, so I can finish). You get the point. My wife and I don't always agree, but we do agree on a good number of issues and "Diversity" is one of them.

Two attractive and intelligent ladies were the instructors for the Diversity portion of the college and they kept emphasizing that everyone wanted to be referred to by their ethnic backgrounds, such as African-Americans, Asia-Americans, Mexican-Americans, etc., etc., etc., you get the point. Jeannie was sitting at a table with some of the other judges and it looked liked a rainbow because there were members of every race at her table. And none of the people were buying into this BS because as they all said, this would create an us vs. them atmosphere in the community. So my wife stood up and asked the instructors what they would classify her as (Jeannie is 5' 6", blond, with green eyes). They both agreed that she was a person of non-color. Jeannie pointed out that she had freckles and one or two moles that were brown, she had a pink tone to her skin, and if she goes out into the sun too long, it turns red. Then she asked the ladies to tell her what label of American she was, to which they said, "Obviously European." She asked them how they knew that when she herself did not have a clue to her family history. Both were a little shocked and ask her what she meant. She told them she did not have a clue to her family background since she was adopted and all of her family history was sealed by court records. So, does that mean we have to add a new category to the Diversity program and call it the Adopted-Americans? If we are going to live in a PC world, would Adopted-Americans have to wear an AA pin so everyone would know who they were, thus ensuring they would not intentionally offend them by addressing them incorrectly? Trust me, when Jeannie sat down she had them scratching their heads with that one.

Fill in the _____ -Americans

"There is no room in this country for hyphenated Americans. The one absolutely certain way of bringing this nation to ruin, of preventing all possibility of it continuing to be a nation at all, would be to permit to become a tangle of squabbling nationalities." ...Theodore Roosevelt, 1915

I have only known one true "African-American" in my life and he is one of the smartest and friendliest young man you will ever meet. I first met Henry Egbuka in graduate school at St. Martin's College in Lacey, Washington. Henry is originally from Nigeria, Africa and lived there the majority of his life. He graduated from college with a degree in Mechanical Engineering and came to the good old USA. He joined the Army for a selfish reason. If this country was willing to let him live here he was willing to protect it with the hopes of someday becoming a US Citizen. He married a beautiful young lady and now has a little boy to add to his family, and he is one of the few people in the country that can truly call themselves "African-American". I have several friends whose ancestors more than likely originated from Africa, but guess what - they all refer to themselves as Black. Imagine that. Someone is referring to themselves in an unpolitically correct manner. Where are the PC Police when you need them?

Yes, there are groups of White people that seem to think that they have to be politically correct creatures too and let's look at a few of these PC groups. We have Irish-Americans, Italian-Americans, Norwegian, Scottish, German, French (this group has not been that vocal since the Iraqi War, unless you count the Coon Asses in Louisiana), along with a host of other groups. It is obvious by now at any given time in

America we can have a parade celebrating some groups' ethnic background. Next, we could cover the group from south of the border, but since I do not want to come off as being a complete un-PC moron, I do not know what the flavor of the month is in regards to what they want to be called. Is it Hispanic-Americans, Latin-Americans, Latino-Americans, Cuban-Americans, Mexican-Americans, etc., etc.? It changes so often we need to be issued a players guide like the type you find at a sporting event, and no, we will not require numbers and names on the backs.

Next we can cover Asian-Americans, Pacific Islander-Americans, Alaska Eskimo-Americans, Native American-Americans, along with a host of other groups the government has on file along with every application you have to fill out. Just think how long it takes a Zimbabwe-American to find the box to check on some government form. It has to be on the bottom of page 254. What is the one common denominator all of the groups have in common? If you have not figured it out let me give all of you "Common Sense Challenged" (ain't being PC correct wonderful at times) people the simple answer, **_AMERICANS!_** And if you cannot read that last word, you are blinder than a bat (and screw the PC police for that last statement). If you are not proud to be an American first, then "Kiss My Red, White and Blue Ass!" If you want to know my family background it is real simple. If my folks had gotten me from a pound instead of the hospital I would be classified a "Mutt" (and yes my parents were married prior to my arrival and I have papers to prove it). My "Pedigree" is a mixture of Welch, Irish, German, and Native American (now you know why I am such a hard-headed opinionated person), along with a host of other groups. And yes, we have some famous as well as infamous people in our family history, but that is a whole other story. Yes, I will drink "Green Beer" on St.

Patty's day, and yes, there have been times when I have drank green beer and it was nowhere close to March 17th. But I do not run around with a bag pipe screaming to the winds the glory of the old country. I have been to Europe several times, but I have never been to Ireland, but one day my wife and I would like to see the country. You see what I am getting at? Yes, when we celebrate these other countries holidays, I can stick out my chest and say I have a family member that is from there and who knows, I may still have family over there. But guess what I was born in Brewton, Alabama, in the United States of America. And that, ladies and gentlemen, truly makes me a Native American.

For all of you enlightened, overly educated, blue-blooded, upper crust and just plain snobs that has to categorize every American with the dreaded dash between two nouns, why don't you describe the groups as American-Irish, American-African, American-Mexican, etc. etc., while the rest of us trod along trying to make a living and learning how to respect our fellow AMERICANS the best way we know how?

History of Politically Correct Language

If you go on the Internet and do a Google search of "Politically Correct" and download every article, joke, story or definition, you could lock up a main frame computer the size of one that NASA uses. So to save all of you the time of looking it up for yourselves, I will give you a "Readers Digest" version. To add insult to injury, the best description I found was written by some foreigner. I will give you the first page and the last paragraph, and if you want to read the entire text, please feel free to look it up.

Politically Correct Language[24]

"The political correctness (PC) movement espouses increasing tolerance, respect and sensitivity for a diversity of race, gender, sexual preference, nationality, religion and even for another's age, physical handicap, alternate lifestyle or any situation or view that might differ from one's own. The aim of the PC movement is to suppress thoughts or statements deemed offensive, prejudicial or stereotypical – anything that might intimidate people or make them feel uneasy." The issue of political correctness has been fiercely debated in the United States, especially during the 1990's. The term "political correctness" mentioned 103 times in American newspapers in 1988, was mentioned 10,000 times only five years later in 1993. It has been said to be merely a college issue, but this hardly the case, as PC seems to be mirrored more and more in real, everyday life of America.

Political correctness as a phenomenon first received widespread publicity in the media in the 1970's when NOW (the National Organization for Women) proposed such language revisions as "chair" or "chairperson" instead of "chairman". However, the Civil Rights movement was way ahead, and had

---

[24] Kaisa Paasivirta, <u>Politically Correct Language</u>, A FAST-US-1 (TRENPP2A) Introduction to American English First Paper, (Department of Translation Studies, University of Tampere), 1998, www.uta.fi/FAST/US1/P1/pckasia.html.

already, in the 1960's, demanded black people to be called "black" instead of "Negro".

(Last paragraph) However, language is by no means an unimportant matter. In my opinion, PCers should be acknowledged by the fact that they have increased the awareness of language as a means of oppression. Language is not "god-given" and thus, can never be untouched by human views, attitudes and prejudice. Therefore, it can also be said that the aims of the PC movement can never be fully achieved. As long as language is produced by human beings, the goals of total neutrality and tolerance will remain unattainable.

Now that the history lesson is over, and, being the lovable smartass that I am, you can rest assured that I will educate the American public in the only way I can. And how is that, you ask? By not giving a damn, if you agree with me or not. If you've read this far, you might as well finish before you start cussing me. Whether you agree or disagree with the following PC statements this is material that will be coming from a good number of other people. So you will see that I am not the last of my species (un-Politically Correct Neanderthal) but there are plenty of people out there wandering around in public all by themselves (the majority of their keepers are government employees, do I need to say more?). But rest assured good PC citizens, the PC police have copied the armed forces in Iraq and issued playing cards with pictures (of course by now you know I would be the ace of spades [you think by now someone would come up with another name for this card since it could be seen as offense, how about Ace of Entrenching Tool]) of all un-PC people. The only problem? There are so many of us un-PC people that the casinos are complaining because the government's order has put their normal orders on the back burners.

"If you have any doubts about the power of political correctness, try asking the Personnel Department (oops – Human Resources) to explain how diversity contributes to better results. Question why reparations make sense when everyone involved is long dead. Ask why people who blow themselves up and kill kids (oops – express their frustrations caused by others) aren't called socialists. Ask some loud-mouthed nut (oops – an advocate or activist) to explain something we are all supposed to accept as true, even when it makes no sense. Or try telling a greenie-weenie (oops – environmentalist) it is better to drill in Anwar than to send billions to Saddam for oil".[25]

Politically Correct Statements Regarding Men[26]

1. He does not have a beer gut; he has developed a LIQUID GRAIN STORAGE FACILITY.
2. He is not quiet; he is a CONVERSATIONAL MINIMALIST.
3. He does not get lost all the time; he DISCOVERS ALTERNATIVE DESTINATIONS.
4. He is not balding; he is in FOLLICLE REGRESSION (also known as a solar panel for a sex machine, this is my description for some of my friends)
5. He does not get falling-down drunk; he becomes ACCIDENTALLY HORIZONTAL.
6. He is not short; he is ANTOMICALLY

---

[25] www.bumperstatements.com, February 17, 2004

[26] www.ajokes.com, February 17, 2004

COMPACT (since I am 6'8" does that make me ANTOMICALLY ENHANCED?)

7. He does not constantly talk about cars; he has a VEHICUI,AR ADDICTION.

8. He does not eat like a pig; he suffers from REVERSE BULIMIA.

9. He is not a bad dancer with no rhythm; he is OVERLY CAUCASIAN.

10. He is not afraid of commitment; he is MONOGAMOUSLY CHALLENGED.

Politically Correct Statements Regarding Schools & Students[27]

1. No one fails a class anymore, he's merely 'PASSING IMPAIRED'.

2. Cheating is no longer cheating, its "COOPERATIVE LEARNING".

3. You don't have detention, you're just one of the "EXIT DELAYED".

4. These days, a student isn't lazy. He's "ENERGETICALLY DECLINED".

5. Kids don't get grounded anymore. They merely hit "SOCIAL SPEED BUMPS".

6. It's not called gossip anymore. It's "THE SPEEDY TRANSMISSION OF NEAR-FACTUAL INFORMATION".

7. You're not being sent to the principal's office. You're "GOING ON A MANDATORY FIELD TRIP TO THE ADMINISTRATIVE BUILDING".

---

[27] www.geocities.com, February 17, 2004

I guess my biggest problem with being politically correct is that there are no true standards for being politically correct. I mean, what is PC today may be un-PC tomorrow. One example is the one group that was called Latino-Americans last month but today are Hispanic-Americans. So how the hell do you expect us "Cavemen" (damn that was stupid, I meant Cavepersons) to get it right if we do not have something in writing (and if it has pictures that would be truly helpful to some of our population)? What I am proposing is a dictionary of PC terms? We all have the ability to look up something in Webster's don't we? And no, this dictionary cannot be changed at will or become the flavor of the day. Once something is placed in the PC dictionary it can only be changed in the same manner as the US Constitution. That means two-thirds of the states will have to adopt the change. With that said the following is a good start for a dictionary. This could become known as "The Bill Of Rights That Corrected The Wrongs." Kind of catchy don't you think? If you do not like it, don't blame me, I did not make it up. I found it on the Internet.

Politically Correct Dictionary[28]

Actor: metamorphosing being, possessing great wealth. **Actress**: metamorphosing being, possessing great wealth (and occasionally great beauty). **Android**: bipedal, non-human associate, bearing immense knowledge and skill. **Bag boy**: agricultural product organizer. **Bald**: follicularly challenged. **Bomb**: vertically deployed antipersonnel device. **Boy**: oppressor-to-be. **Brainwashing**: cognitive accommodation. **Cafeteria**: dining facility. **Car**: earth-unfriendly, vertically-challenged mode of transport. **Car Wash Worker**: vehicle-appearance specialist. **Cat**: quadruped non-human associate.

---

[28] www.funny2.com/dictionary.htm, February 20, 2004

Cheating: cooperative assignment.   **Computer**: machine bearing immense power and fallibility. **Criticism**: unjust self-esteem reducer. **Dead**: metabolically challenged. **Demand**: propose strongly. **Derision**: nontraditional praise. **Dirty Old Man**: sexually focused, chronologically gifted individual. **Dumb**: cerebrally challenged.   **Evil**: niceness deprived. **Exercise**: body enhancement through exertion. **Failure**: nontraditional success. **Fart**: human ozone depletor; ecologically incorrect expression.   **Fat**: horizontally challenged: person of substance.   **Garbage collector**: sanitation engineer. **Gas Station Attendant**: petroleum transfer technician. **Girl**: pre-woman.   **Guess**: anomaly maneuvers: repetitive predictions. **Handicapped**: physically challenged.   **Heroine**: hera. **Homeless person:** residentially flexible individual. **Hurricane**: himmicane (non sexist). **Ignorant:** factually unencumbered. **Incorrect**: alternative answer. **Individualism**: uncooperative spirit. **Information**: overly structured trivia. **Insane**: reality challenged.   **Kill**: creating a permanent state of metabolic dormancy; servicing the target (military). **Lazy**: motivationally dispossessed. **Lost:** locationally disadvantaged. **Man:** oppressor. **Manhole**: maintenance portal. **Misunderstand**: personalized interpretation.   **Monster**: person of scales.   **Mugging**: unforeseen funding of underclass. **Murderer**: termination specialist. **Nerd**: under-attractive, cerebrally gifted individual. **Numismatist**: capitalist monetary acquisition expert. **Nut**: hexagonal rotatable surface compression unit. **Off**: energy efficient. **Old**: chronologically gifted. **Perfume**: discretionary fragrance. **Pervert:** person engaged in nontraditional espionage. **Pissed off**: satisfaction deprived.   **Political**: amorally gifted. **Poor**: economically marginalized.   **Prisoner**: client of the correctional system. **Prostitute**: body entrepreneur. **Redneck:** rustically inclined. **Rich**: economically maximized. **Secretary**: stationery engineer. **Sex**: cooperative physical fitness. **Sexist**: gender biased with niceness deprived overtones.   **Short**:

altitudinally disadvantaged: vertically challenged. **Sleepy**: under-alert. **Smart**: cerebrally gifted. **Specialist**: physician having concentrated on a particular field of tax shelters. **Structure**: impersonal hindrance. **Tall**: vertically gifted: altitudinally endowed. **Teacher**: volunteer knowledge conveyor. **Teaching**: personality repression. **Television**: medium of electrons moving in disorganized patterns. **Tired**: rest-challenged. **Uglier**: over under-attractive. **Ugliest**: over-under-attractively gifted. **Ugly**: under-attractive. **Unemployed**: non-waged. **Unsure**: conceptual conflict. **Waiter**: waitron. **Waitress**: waitron. **White**: melanin-impoverished; member of the mutant albino genetic-recessive global minority. **Woman**: w/o man; womyn. **Zipper**: interlocking slide fasteners

An Un-PC American

The person I am going to describe below is a controversial artist that has made the "Righties" stand up and cheer along with a good majority of us "Middle Of the Roaders" (MOR). And he truly pisses off the Lefties a hell'va a lot better than I could ever hope to do. I do not know his political leaning, but I have more respect for him than any politician because of the respect he shows for our service men and women. 60 Minutes did a show on him and one line of questioning was regarding his "Taliban" song making fun of an Al Quaida member. "Don't you think this is harmful and discriminating to Middle East-Americans?" This is coming from the same news anchor that would not allow any of his reporters to wear a US flag pin on their lapels. The man basically told him that if you are against the US this song may piss you off good. If you are sensitive and have your feelings easily hurt, turn off the radio.

Toby Keith

CCP # F150 (Ford Truck Commercial) is a Country superstar and a very patriotic American. For all of you CCPs that do not listen to country music, you may have heard of this young man because of his controversial song "Courtesy of the Red, White and Blue (The Angry American)". Personally, I do not understand what is so controversial about the song because it basically states the truth. He states in the song that if you come over here and harm us, then we, and I am quoting, "are going to put a boot up your ass". Now if he is not telling the truth, why did this song make him so much money? And the greatest compliment I can think of was when the POWs were released, the story told by the majority of the POWs said one of them in the group kept singing this song and was really pissing off his captors. It was also stated that his singing left a lot to be desired and he was starting to piss off the other POWs.

Mr. Keith did not originally write this song for September 11, 2001. It was written for his father who had died in a car wreck six months prior. His father was U.S. Army veteran H. K. Covel and in the song, it says he lost his right eye in the army but he flew his flag up to the day he died. Here is more proof that the apple does not fall far from the tree. Toby put to music what the majority of CCPs of this country feel and are damn proud of him for singing it. It seems to me if the "Rag heads" (the politically correct police informed me that the cloth that the Middle-Easterners wear on their head is not a rag, but a small sheet, so from this time on, Rag Heads will be referred to as Sheet Heads) had read the history books, they could have saved themselves a lot of pain and suffering. Note to future Sheet Heads about to attack the U.S.: when you are in the library looking up places to attack, look in the history books and reference December 7, 1941, and see what took place the following four years.

Toby was to perform on a Peter Jennings special that was celebrating the 4th of July in 2002. A few days after he received the invitation, it was rescinded because the lyrics were "objectionable". All this did was put a spotlight on the song and helped launch it to the top of the charts. Toby, I hope you sent Peter a thank you note, and you did not need to be seen with him anyway. You know your parents taught you better, remember that lesson, "Be careful who you hang around with?" If you hang around that transplanted Canadian you would not want to have any US flags around you either. I am not trying to offend our Canadian CCPs because I know a lot of good people north of our border from all of the years I worked up there. It is just that I have no love lost for the news-readers of our country.

Then here comes, the other bombshell that Toby has had to toy with. Toby weren't you listening when your mama or granny told you it is not fair having a battle of the wits with an unarmed person? Ms. Natallie Maines of the Dixie Chicks took offense of the Red, White, and Blue lyrics and then she really got her panties in a wad when Toby displayed her picture with Saddam Hussein's at his concerts. Okay son, let's look at the facts. Wherever you go, you state your beliefs, and if the people do not like this attitude, they damn sure wouldn't like the next one. If you are interviewed by Barbara Walters, you will not dance around the questions and make a half-assed excuse for what you said. On the other hand, Maines is overseas when she makes the statement about the President. I agree that she has the right to say whatever she wants. The First Amendment of the Constitution gives her that right. But if she is so high and mighty, let's see if she has the balls to make the same statement in downtown DALLAS. Next, she shows up at one of her concerts wearing a tee shirt that says F.U.T.K. It is not that she is mad at you, she just wants your body. She is playing hard to get. You have heard that old saying, "Treat a stud like a dud and a dud like a stud and they are like putty in your hand". That's all she is trying to do. If you think I am pulling you leg, the next time your tour comes near Dr. Phil's studio, stop in for a session and you will see, he will agree with me. Mr. Keith, thank you for your music and I am sorry you recently lost your father. You are one CCP that I would like to be able to call a friend, along with the majority of the CCPs in the US.

The next two people you are going to read about will show you proof that the majority of Americans are un-PC creatures themselves. If they were truly PC then these guys' careers would have never taken off and both of them are huge in the entertainment industry. Week after week we watch people being verbally abused by these un-PC knuckle draggers and we agree with everything they say.

Dr. Phil

CCP #72 (since he is an avid golfer this may be the only time he comes close to par), I know why he is hair challenged! All those years he practiced before he came on Oprah's show he had to be politically correct to his patients. After watching some of the idiots (future Darwin Award candidates) he has had on his show, you know they are some of the same ones he saw in private practice, thus the only thing he could do was to pull his hair out. Now that he is on TV he can be as rude, crude and socially unacceptable as he wants to be, and the best part is that these people are lining up to come on his show to be humiliated to millions on TV. To me it looks as if some of these people are Jerry Springer rejects, but just found better clothes at the Goodwill store. I am quoting from Dr. Phil's web site, "After years of practicing, Dr. Phil realized that traditional therapy was not his calling. From the very beginning, it wasn't for me. I didn't have the patience for it, he says". Maybe I was right in the first chapter when I described him as the "Drive-Thru Psycho Psychiatrist". You know it had to be comforting to his patients when he was consulting them and they would catch him looking at his watch. Did he give his patients a discount if the session did not last a full hour?

I was not a fan of Dr. Phil at first, but he has won me over in several areas. When he appeared on David Letterman's show and shot zingers one-for-one at Dave, it was great. What impressed me was that David has all of these writers giving him his material, and Dr. Phil looked like Rambo firing a M-60 at a paper target. David was doing some serious "Crawfishing" (if you do not know what that means, ask one of your southern friends to explain it to you) to Dr. Phil. And then before Dr. Phil left the stage, David started whining about Oprah again, wanting to know if she ever mentioned his name and did he think he could get him on Oprah's show. Damn Dave, we know you got a set of balls; you just announced that your girl friend had your first child, so ball check time. Just show up at Oprah's front door and walk on stage. What is she going to say? Then again, if you had help in producing the baby you had better wait for an invitation. The second thing that impresses me about Dr. Phil is his work ethics. He is becoming the Steven King of the self-help industry and he has his own show. He still appears on Oprah's show occasionally and he conducts motivational seminars across the country. Could this be why he does not put up with any of the B.S. from the people on his show, and why he jumps in their asses with both feet? Do the following two words mean anything to you Dr. Phil: Sleep Deprivation?

What I want to know is what does he have that I don't? Other than a Doctorate degree and millions of dollars, that is. I mean, for years I have been telling people what to do, where to go and what their problems were. And at times I have been as pushy, rude, obnoxious and as opinionated as Dr. Phil. Let's look at the similarities between the two of us. 1) We are both originally from the South (we were taught all those good manners and neither one of us used them on a regular basis), 2) We are both ex-football players (maybe all of the pains from old injuries gives us our sparkling personalities), 3) We are both dapper dressers, and 4) I have hair on the top of my head and he has hair over his top lip. I ask you again, what does he have that I don't?

Simon Cowell

CCP # 50,000,000 (this number has a direct relationship to the amount of money he has supposedly made with the American Idol enterprise): and yes, he has the same first name as that literature villain Simon Lagree, along with the same mentality. Yes, he is one of them foreigners and we Americans know all foreigners are rude and uncivilized. And being reared in the manner and atmosphere of their upbringing, how could we ever expect them to reach the lofty heights of PC Utopia?

"A&E Biography" recently did an episode on him and was telling about one of the first American Idol auditions to take place with Paula Abdul and Randy Jackson. Now you have to remember that Paula and Randy live in the Mecca of the PC universe, Los Angeles. This is the land where people would rather have a skin peel done with a steel wool pad than be accused of being un-PC and intentionally hurting someone's feelings. This group of people has never understood that old expression, "The truth hurts" and they continue to let people lie to themselves. When the first contestant came in to sing to the judges, Simon stopped the guy in the middle of the song and told him how horrible he was as only Simon can. Paula immediately went into cardiac arrest and the PC paramedics had to rip open her blouse (lucky guys) and apply the defibrillator pads to shock her back to life. The first thing she said after she recovered from the shock (figurative not literal) was "you can't talk to Americans like that" and why the hell not? Simon was only looking out for the production company. Coming to America, he learned of all the rules and regulations that we have to live with and he is worried about the EPA fining him for noise pollution. The first guy was atrocious and that is putting it lightly, if this audition had taken place in the Vaudeville days the hook would have come out and they would have been aiming for the "family jewels" to ensure he did not breed, thus keeping him from carrying on the family tradition of not being able to sing. In some third world nations they would have taken him out back and shot him. And all Simon did was to tell him he sucked and could not sing. How many years do you think family and friends had to put up with this guys screeching, while all along, he thinks he is great? Personally, I do not feel bad for the family and friends for having to put up with this agony if they did not have the balls to tell him how bad he was. Oh, how knuckle dragging of me. By telling this little clown how bad he is, we could hurt his precious psyche and God knows what wrath he would unleash on society. He could become a serial killer, a mass murderer, a child molester, or a US Congressman. See, the potential is unlimited. And all Simon did was put him on another path of life in an un-PC manner.

Simon is not all bad. He is looking out for some of the contestant's personal safety. Example: one young lady that tried out was a member of the US Army, and I believe she was with the 82nd Airborne (I not sure of the number, but I do know it was Airborne). After she sang, Randy and Paula critiqued her performance and let her down as softly as one of the parachutes she uses. Simon's turn, "Contestant's Name whatever you do for God's sake, do not ever sing to the guy that packs your parachute". Now what was wrong with that statement? He was truly looking out for the young lady's health. Let's face it; all of you PC socialites. When you hear one of these kids sounding like a jet engine starting up with a couple of fan blades missing, you say some discouraging remarks to the TV. And don't try to tell me you run to the PC church and go to PC confessional to redeem you from your sinful transaction. You smile and agree whole heartedly with Simon and deep down you are jealous of him (I'm not talking about his money) that he is man enough to tell these people to their faces that they stink.

Randy Jackson was quoted on the same show saying that "Simon has two shirts and wears his pants too high". Okay, he likes black T-shirts. Don't all villains wear black? Or maybe he is trying for the Don Johnson look from Miami Vice, without the jacket. And what is with the pants. Are you practicing for when you retire and move to South Florida? You will be in style with all of those old men that wear their pants so high the belts are under their armpits and the zippers are at their sternums. Lighten up guys, you have enough money. You can quit shopping at the Goodwill store. I thought about sending your name into the "Queer Eye for the Straight Guy" show, but I figure the strain in emergency rooms in Los Angeles is over worked all ready, and you would obviously send all of those guys into trauma with your un-PC attitude. So I did the next best thing, I put your name in for the show "What Not To Wear." Since they are as tactful as you, it would be a threesome made in heaven.

Maybe Governor Terminator (Arnold) is correct. It is time for a change, and foreign-born people should be allowed to run for President. Can't you see it now? President Cowell's first "State of the Union" address, the pictures coming from the Capitol would remind you of the scene from Jim Jones' Jonestown with bodies lying everywhere. President C tells Congress what a bunch of hypocrites they are and that is just the beginning of the speech, and they start falling like deadwood. One can only hope.

If you have not guessed by now, I think this politically correct movement is a load of BULL (maybe we can get the EPA to investigate while they are looking into all of the dairy farmers). And here is how I will prove my point. The media has bombarded our younger generation with this PC movement. Common sense has left the building along with Elvis. Here is my perfect example. My wife and I recently became guardian of a seventeen-year-old young lady by the name of Brandie. One night she and I were watching the news (truly a slow night). I do not remember the entire story line, but it involved the death of a man from one of the islands somewhere near the British Virgin Islands or the Bahamas. When she asked me a question regarding the story, the first words out of her mouth describing the man was "African-American". I looked at her and said the man was not an American. Then she got a confused look on her face and then asked me, "What should I call him"? I said, "try black." Good God Almighty, you would have thought I had used the N-WORD. How barbaric of me, I was being uncaring and rude describing the man, then I hit her with a question that truly confused her. How can the man be "African-American" when he is not an American? I was not being disrespectful, just truthful. So here is my question to those people who walk around with their noses up in the air (isn't it hard to have you nose up in the air when your head is up your ass?). Are we supposed to call every black person in the world an African-American?

I know I have rambled on for a long time now and you will be glad to hear there is only one more chapter before the end of the book. I will be writing another edition to this one in the future, so if you have something you want investigated,

(Area 51 is off limits; even the alien members have had to sign a confidential agreement with the government), discussed or just plain bitched about, feel free to contact me and I will see what I can do.

13. "CAN'T WE ALL GET ALONG"

> *"If you live to be a hundred, I want to live to be a hundred minus one day, so I never have to live without you."* - *Winnie the Pooh*

If you live long enough and you get through the school of hard knocks you can look back at some of your mistakes, some of your victories and some of your not-so-glorious moments. Maybe you would have changed some things, maybe not. But the following are some learning experiences from some fellow CCPs:

Great Truths About Life That Little Children Have Learned:

1. No matter how hard you try, you can't baptize cats.
2. When your mom is mad at your dad, don't let her brush your hair.
3. If your sister hits you, don't hit her back. They always catch the second person.
4. Never ask your three-year-old brother to hold a tomato.
5. You can't trust dogs to watch your food.

6. Don't sneeze when someone is cutting your hair.
7. Never hold a Dust Buster and a cat at the same time.
8. You can't hide a piece of broccoli in a glass of milk.
9. Don't wear polka dot underwear under white shorts.
10. The best place to be when you're sad is Grandpa's lap.

Great Truths About Life That Adults Have Learned:

1. Raising teenagers is like nailing Jell-O to a tree.
2. Wrinkles don't hurt.
3. Families are like fudge, mostly sweet, with a few nuts.
4. Today's mighty oak is just yesterday's nut that held its ground.
5. Laughing is good exercise. It's like jogging on the inside.
6. Middle age is when you choose your cereal for the fiber, not the joy.

Great Truths About Growing Old:

1. Growing old is mandatory, growing up is optional.
2. Forget the health food. I need all the preservatives I can get.
3. When you fall down, you wonder what else you can do while you're down there.
4. You're getting old when you get the same sensation from a rocking chair that you once got from a roller coaster.
5. It's frustrating when you know all the answers, but nobody bothers to ask you the questions.

6. Time may be a great healer, but it's a lousy beautician.

7. Wisdom comes with age, but sometimes age comes alone.

The Four Stages Of Life:

1. You believe in Santa Claus.
2. You don't believe in Santa Claus.
3. You are Santa Claus.
4. You look like Santa Claus.

Success:

- At age 4   success is   not peeing in your pants
- At age 12   success is   having friends
- At age 16   success is   having a drivers license
- At age 20   success is   having sex
- At age 35   success is   having money
- At age 50   success is   having money
- At age 60   success is   having sex
- At age 70   success is   having a drivers license
- At age 75   success is   having friends
- At age 80   success is   not peeing in your pants

I wish I could say that I was the person who summed up our time on this planet with those profound words of wisdom, Great Truths About Life and The Four Stages of Life and Success. I wish I could acknowledge who wrote these words of wisdom that will surely be true through the annals of time, but I cannot since these immortal words were sent to me via e-mail. But the author should know, if and when the organization of CCPs erect a Hall of Fame, these words will be found on a plaque at the entrance of the building.

Ccp Command Modules (Recliners)

Every card carrying CCP knows that every home is lacking if it does not have a recliner, aka "The Command Module." Most of us CCPs, upon leaving the nest and getting our first apartments, did not have much money to spend on furniture and could not afford a command module. So we did the next best thing. We bought a beanbag chair. I know it is not the real deal, but at being such a young age, we may not have been ready for the full-blown module. If a recliner is a Harley Davidson, think of the beanbag as a Moped. Everyone has to learn to walk before they run. Once you have a little extra money and you are ready for the command module, go for it, you can go for a used one from a second hand shop or a garage sale. No one will think badly of you, because we have all been in your shoes. But in this day and age of furniture, they have command modules that have phones, heating areas, massages, and other options that will make it hard for you to get up to go to bed or that dirty word, WORK. For some of you upper level CCPs, here are some of the hottest command modules that money can buy, and if the spouse is not wild about such caveman furniture, they will be delighted since these new products are so avant-garde.

1. Archie Bunker wouldn't touch the Deco-inspired **Carlyle** from **La-Z-Boy**. But Edith might. The sleek seat is elegant, graceful and more comfortable than it looks, and its scaled-down proportions accommodate a more slender frame, making it a perfect lounger for the lady of the house. It's also easier to open than many of its oversize counterparts. Oh Archie! **Cost:** About $650.[29]

---

[29]   "Insider," TV Guide, (April 5, 2003): 15.

2.   The **Joey Recliner** from **Mitchell Gold** is named for - guess who? The recliner-loving character on NBC's hit Friends. Sure, it may look like a dapper 1950s-style club chair. But don't let its high fashion fool you. In full recumbent mode, this glove soft, densely cushioned lounger would please the Baywatch taping inner Joey of every man. **Cost:** About $2,500.[30]

3.   **Barcalounger's** rugged **Crossroads** recliner is a tribute to testosterone. Its distressed leather is soft but masculine. The seat is cut deep for long, manly legs, and kicking back requires a firm push on the arms. Heck, even the anti-recliner Frazier wouldn't mind having this hunk of comfort in the house. **Cost:** About $1,900.[31]

4.   Talk about a hot seat! The **Panasonic Shiatsu Massage Lounger** boasts powerful remote-control operated massage nodes that knead, and roll their way up and down the entire back, producing the kind of euphoria that could make a spouse jealous. Of course, reclining the old-fashioned way without the massage is also an option. But why do that? **Cost:** About $3,195.[32]

IS THIS A GREAT COUNTRY OR WHAT? ONLY IN AMERICA! I informed my wife that I would like to get the Panasonic Lounger for my birthday and she said and I quote, "Yeah Right." So what do you think my chances are?

For all of us baby boomers that grew up watching television early in the morning before going off to school, we had our

---

[30]   "Insider," TV Guide, (April 5, 2003): 15.

[31]   Ibid.

[32]   "Insider," TV Guide, (April 5, 2003): 15.

favorite heroes and TV personalities. The following story is very true in respect to the title.

Never Judge A Book By Its Cover.

This was a dialogue from a Johnny Carson's "Tonight Show" and Johnny's guest that night was Lee Marvin. Johnny said, "Lee, I'll bet a lot of people are unaware that you were a Marine in the initial landing at Iwo Jima and that during the course of that action, you earned the Navy Cross and were severely wounded." Lee Marvin's response was, "Yeah, yeah, I got shot square in the ass and they gave me the Cross for securing a hot spot about halfway up Mount Suribachi. The bad thing about getting shot up on a mountain is the guys getting shot hauling you down. But Johnny, at Iwo, I served under the bravest man I ever knew. We both got the Cross the same day, but what he did for his Cross made mine look cheap in comparison. The dumb bastard actually stood up on Red Beach and directed his troops to move forward and get the hell off the beach. That Sergeant and I have been life-long friends. When they brought me off Suribachi, we passed him and he lit a smoke and passed it to me lying on my belly on the litter. 'Where'd they get you Lee?' he asked. 'Well Bob, they shot me in the ass and if you make it home before me, tell Mom to sell the outhouse'. Johnny, I'm not lying, Sergeant Keeshan was the bravest man I ever knew!" Johnny said, "You now know him as Bob Keeshan." Lee replied, "You and the world know him as 'Captain Kangaroo'."

What Happened To The World I Grew Up In?

By now all of you know I am one of the "Baby Boomers" that was born in the 50's, when life was simpler. But it sure as hell wasn't grand and were they truly the good old days?

Yes, there were two parents in the majority of the homes in America, but that does not mean everyone was living in an Ozzie and Harriet world, and you can bet your sweet ass that there were not too many Ozzy Osborne families known to the public. The Osborne family is definitely the poster child for the old statement that said, "They put the *fun* in the word Dys**fun**ctional." If I had ever been dumb enough, drunk enough, or just plain brain dead or had balls enough to speak to my parents in the manner in which the Osborne kids do, the odds are very good that today I would not have the ability to have written this book. My Dad would have drop kicked my ass through the sliding glass door and that would have been just to get my attention. I received five spankings from my father in my lifetime (today some people would call it child abuse) and trust me, to this day, I can remember every one of them. All my mother had to say was "I'm going to tell your dad" and you can bet you life I quit whatever I was doing. If she had told me to stop the world from turning I would have found a brake and one half of the world would be in a constant state of darkness to this day. On the other hand, if I had a dime for every spanking I received from Mom, I would be able to balance the U.S. budget.

Down South when you got into trouble, the parents used to make the kids go outside and pick the weapon that was going to be used against them for punishment. "Go outside and get me a switch to whip you with." The majority of the children thought these words were part of the 10 Commandments from the Bible. For all of you non-southerners, a switch can be found on most bushes basically it is a limb from said bush. The requirements of a switch are 1) Long, 2) very, very, very flexible. And like most of the kids, I would go outside and find the longest and thinnest switch I could find, then I would come back in the house groveling, more like crying and sniffling, and praying to God, Allah, Buddha, or any other deity (I was trying to cover all of the bases) that if he would spare me from this beating, I would never do that act again (unless it was kicking my brother's butt, God knows that is the law of nature). As usual there was no divine intervention, so I would have to hand over the switch to my mother who would in turn swing the weapon through the air to see if it met the U.S. ass-whipping specifications. The way that switch could sing going through the air sometimes made you think your Mother was related to Zorro (for all you "Baby Boomers" don't try to tell me you do not know who Zorro was). She did not draw blood, I did not have to go to the ER, and you can take it for granted, I did not do that same offense for a while (unless it involved beating on Ricky). If I knew then what I know now, I would have gone outside and found a six foot 4"x4" fence post and drug it back to the house and given it to Mom. I would have liked to have seen her swing that bad boy. And switches were not found only at my home, they had the bad habit of growing all over the South.

My maternal Grandmother's (Granny) home was completely surrounded by flower beds and these flower beds were filled with old growth Azaleas. In the Spring, Granny's house was picture perfect with all of the blooming Azaleas. By the end of the summer it looked as if a swarm of locusts had come through the yard. My cousin, Wewa, and I would stay at Granny's for weeks at a time in the summer and we have been called on more than one occasion "Agitate and Aggravate." I think we were 16 years old before we found out that those descriptions were not our middle names. Funny, how you remember little things like this in your later years of life. Yes, Granny would fan our little asses when we were out of line, and guess what? Wewa and I didn't become mass murders, gang bangers, child molesters, or any other psychological degenerate. On this one I am speaking for myself, sometimes I am not to sure about Wewa. Neither one of us has ever been arrested, if the truth was known, we just weren't caught for some of our antics, both have jobs, raised families and helped our communities become a better place to live.

I'm not saying that beating children is the correct way to raise children, but this "Time Out" crap and "Let's have a philosophical discussion with little Johnny/Suzy to discuss what we did wrong" isn't working. I sure wish my parents had read Dr. Spock instead of that verse in the Bible that says "Spare the rod; Spoil the child."

A few years ago I read a bumper sticker that said "Remember when the air was clean and sex was dirty." The bad thing about this day and age is that both of these items can kill you. Today just about everything a person does will eventual kill them, breathing (air pollution), sex (HIV, AIDS, jealous spouses), eating (mercury in fish, mad cow disease, vegetables with pesticides, etc.), work (stress)... Why do people want to bring children in this world? Why do people want to continue to live? I do not know about the majority of you, but I am going to stick around just to piss off a bunch of people.

I do not know of a single family when I was young that had an Ozzie and Harriet lifestyle. Hell, even the real Ozzie and Harriet family did not live the lifestyle they portrayed on TV. History has shown that Ozzie (we know today's Ozzy hasn't got a clue as to what I am talking about) was not the all American Dad that he orchestrated. Yes, every family had skeletons in their closets, and some of the closets could fill up an entire cemetery. What was the secret to the "All American Family?" Well, first of all, there was no true "All American Family", but families did communicate more than they do today. In most households the dinner table was an important part of the house, and when dinner was served the TV was turned OFF. Families actually talked with each other. They didn't leave a voice mail, e-mail, or any other type of electronic message. Maybe if some of today's families would try this concept this could help solve some of their problems. Just remember, talk is cheap, unless you're talking to a lawyer.

So where did we "Baby Boomer" CCPs go wrong? Is it our fault that today's society has the same amount of common sense as an amoeba? The Political Correctness movement - Is this where the world started going to hell in a hand basket? Where is it written that it is the government's job to ensure that no one in the country ever has their feelings hurt, or they get a job or position even if they are not qualified for the position and that we will all live happily ever after. It does not work that way in nature, everyone has heard of "The Law of the Jungle" and "Only The Strong Survive." So when did the government or the people in academia decide that they were more powerful than God or nature and could change the status of human nature and evolution. Sorry for that last sentence. I was getting in touch with my Neanderthal side.

Who was the idiot that first made the statement "The older you get, the wiser you are?" Maybe it should read "The older you get, the more you forget what you did when you were young." My prime example has to do with sex education, birth control and the availability of condoms. How many times has this discussion brought on heated arguments from both sides of the political aisle? And what really pushes my hot button is to be in a discussion with a pompous, self-righteous person that has found religion. Anyway, I know what a majority of them were like, and more importantly, what they did when they were younger. When I was a kid, my Mother had me in church every time the doors were open and, to this day, I carry my beliefs close to my heart and it is no one's business how or when I communicate with the Big Man Upstairs (sorry N.O.W., but I believe God's a man). In this day and age, with HIV, AIDS, Herpes, along with a host of other diseases (will someone fill me in when VD became STD, because I missed that part of my life) and teenage pregnancy is rising faster than the rocket that launches the Space Shuttle, what is wrong with trying to protect our children? And let's not forget that when these teenagers are pregnant, those do gooders are the same people who are screaming against abortion. This option is out of the question in their eyes. The people screaming the loudest against abortion are the same ones that will fight the hardest to get the child out of the birth canal. However, at the same time, they're not willing to have one penny of their tax money spent to help support that same child after he/she drops into the doctor's hands. As we all know by now, it has been well documented throughout this book that I am not the smartest person in the world. Hell, I am not even the smartest person in my household. But to me, it looks like the scene described above is an enigma. For us dummies, that means a vicious circle. Education and prevention will not stop all pregnancies and abortions, but it might put a crimp on the numbers. Since the dawn of time when kids' hormones started running rampant, kids and adults have been having sex and guess what? Nothing we say is going to change that. God knows my mother tried, along with several of my friends' parents with them. Funny how kids find the things they need to have fun. There were no clinics that passed out condoms when I was a teenager, but every boy in Pensacola knew that Thoni's Gas Station in the fork of Highway 29 and Old Palifox had a rubber machine in the men's bathroom. And if you were late getting there on a Friday night, more than likely it would be empty. I admit I put my share of quarters in the machine, along with <u>the majority of my friends</u>. The difference between my friends and myself is I am willing to admit I was trying to wear out the shock absorbers on my '67 Mercury Cougar. The majority of my friends seem to have forgotten this part of their lives. Is it because they are having "Senior Moments," dementia, onset stages of Alzheimer's or maybe I got it right the first time... they are a bunch of pompous asses.

One of the best examples of this is our own President of the United States, George W. Bush. In college it seems George W. had a reputation for being a party animal, and now he wants to preach virtues to the American public. If President Bush was a virgin at the time he married Mrs. Bush, then I am back on the moon being a valet again, waiting for the next rover to show up.

Whether the rest of the world likes us - who gives a damn? I know that the majority of the CCPs in the U.S. do not care what the world thinks. It is the politicians, academia, and corporations that value world opinion. With over 200 million CCPs in the states, our opinion should count the most. No, we will never get everyone in America to agree on any one idea or thing, hell most of the time you can't get your own family to agree on what television show to watch. How do we expect to get the country to agree on anything? That is why we are a Republic, where the majority rules. I might not agree with what you are saying, but I agree that you have the right to say it in public. Is this a great country or what? That is enough rambling about my world and lack of wisdom, so just continue reading the last couple of pages to see my suggestions for fixing these problems.

The End At Last!

One day, I was sitting at the Rusty Tractor, a restaurant in Elma, WA,. An elderly gentleman walked into the restaurant, and a friend asked him how he was doing, and the gentleman replied, "I am on this side of the grass." Remember, this is one of the criteria for being a card carrying CCP. Footnote: At time of printing, this rule for being alive is being reviewed by CCP management. The reason for this is due to the fact that one may possibly continue to stay in contact with this world in the after-life because of the following two shows: 1)

Crossing Over with John Edwards, and 2) Beyond with James Van Praugh.

I hope everyone had a good laugh at my view of the world, and I know that I did not please everyone, but that was not my main objective. I just wanted everyone to think about something other than their own selves or their particular view of the world. We are definitely the most diversified country in the world and constantly have strife within our own borders, and maybe, if everyone would sit down with their neighbor and have a cup of coffee, things may change. Do you even know your neighbor's name? Maybe if everyone would live by the following statements the world could be a better place.

Everything I need to know about life, I learned from Noah's Ark.

1. Don't miss the boat.
2. Remember that we are all in the same boat.
3. Plan ahead. It wasn't raining when Noah built the Ark.
4. Stay fit. When you're 600 years old, someone may ask you to do something really big.
5. Don't listen to critics; just get on with the job that needs to be done.
6. Build your future on high ground.
7. For safety's sake, travel in pairs.
8. Speed isn't always an advantage. The snails were on board with the cheetahs.
9. When you're stressed, float a while.
10. Remember, the Ark was built by amateurs; the Titanic by professionals.
11. No matter the storm, when you are with God, there's always a rainbow waiting.

Life

When the door of happiness closes, another opens; but often times we look so long at the closed door that we don't see the one which has been opened for us.

Don't go for looks ; they can deceive. Don't go for wealth; even that fades away. Go for someone who makes you smile, because it takes only a smile to make a dark day seem bright. Find the one that makes your heart smile.

Dream what you want to dream; go where you want to go, be what you want to be, because you have only one life and one chance to do all the things you want to do.

May you have enough happiness to make you sweet, enough trials to make you strong, enough sorrow to keep you human, enough hope to make you happy. The happiest of people don't necessarily have the best of everything; they just make the most of everything that comes along their way.

The brightest future will always be based on a forgotten past; you can't go forward in life until you let go of your past failures and heartaches.

When you were born, you were crying and everyone around you was smiling. Live your life so at the end, you're the one who is smiling and everyone around you is crying.

Life is not measured by the number of breaths we take, but by the moments that take our breath away.

I want to thank CCP #1973 Cindy Peake of Pensacola, FL, for Noah's Ark list and Life's Moments. I hope to see everyone soon, and don't worry; I am still on this side of the grass.

Epilog.

Recently I just purchase a new radio system for my pickup truck and it's name is
Sirus. After the installer finished attaching the system to my dash the first thing he handed me was a remote control.

IS THIS A GREAT COUNTRY OR WHAT?